D1497955

George Henry Boker

Twayne's United States Authors Series

David J. Nordloh, Editor

Indiana University, Bloomington

TUSAS 476

GEORGE HENRY BOKER
(1823–1890)
Photograph courtesy of the
Photographic Archives of the
Union League of Philadelphia

George Henry Boker

By Oliver H. Evans

Twayne Publishers • *Boston*

George Henry Boker

Oliver H. Evans

Copyright © 1984 by G. K. Hall & Company
All Rights Reserved
Published by Twayne Publishers
A Division of G. K. Hall & Company
70 Lincoln Street
Boston, Massachusetts 02111

Book Production by Elizabeth Todesco
Book Design by Barbara Anderson

Printed on permanent/durable acid-free
paper and bound in the United States of
America.

Library of Congress Cataloging in
Publication Data

Evans, Oliver H.
  George Henry Boker.

  (Twayne's United States authors series; TUSAS 476)
  Bibliography: p. 145
  Includes index.
  1. Boker, George H. (George Henry), 1823–1890—
Criticism and interpretation.   2. Boker, George H.
(George Henry), 1823–1890.   Francesca da Rimini.
3. Francesca, da Rimini, d. ca. 1285, in fiction,
drama, poetry, etc.   I. Title.   II. Series.
PS1106.E9   1984   812'.3   84–10871
ISBN 0–8057–7417–3

For Eileen

Contents

About the Author

Oliver H. Evans graduated from Albion College (Michigan) in 1966 with a B.A. in English. He then completed his M.A. and Ph.D. at Purdue University, with a doctoral dissertation, directed by Darrel Abel, on American poetry. His publications include articles in *The Fitzgerald-Hemingway Annual, Shakespeare Studies, Educational Theatre Journal, Pennsylvania Magazine of History and Biography,* and *Texas Studies in Literature and Language.* He is married and has two children, Rachel and Ethan.

Preface

Despite the work earlier in this century of Joseph Wood Krutch, Arthur Hobson Quinn, and Edward Sculley Bradley, the nineteenth-century American poet and playwright George Henry Boker is remembered today, if at all, primarily as the author of *Francesca da Rimini*. The neglect of Boker is not entirely unwarranted. He is not, as were Melville and Dickinson, a major figure waiting to be rescued from obscurity. He is a minor writer, even something of a curiosity in American literature. His life spanned most of the nineteenth century, and his major works were written during that remarkable time which, thanks to F. O. Matthiessen, has come to be thought of as the "American Renaissance." Yet Boker's major works are verse dramas that imitate those of Shakespeare and love sonnets in the style of the Elizabethans. What is one to make of an American writer who during the age of Emerson turned his eyes not only to England, but to sixteenth-century England, for his literary models? Compared with the major nineteenth-century writers, Boker seems an "American" writer only because he was born in this country.

In the past critics hostile to Boker have dismissed him for having failed to see that the day of listening to "the courtly muses" was gone. Those critics, on the other hand, who wished to make a case for Boker usually accepted his own argument that the realm of literature transcends the present and that by looking to the past for his models he was attempting to create a literature that escaped provincialism and had a universal scope. As a result, whether hostile or sympathetic to Boker, critics have ignored the intricacies of his relationship with American literary history, concentrating, at best, on Boker's place in the history of American drama.

There is an advantage to treating Boker solely within the

context of American drama, for among the likes of John Howard Payne, Robert Montgomery Bird, and John Augustus Stone, Boker shines as he can never shine in the company of Emerson, Whitman, Melville, and Hawthorne. But to approach Boker as a writer who in a significant way lies outside the main stream of American literary history is as mistaken as believing that his accomplishment is limited to *Francesca da Rimini.* Boker did not think to himself as a playwright, but as a poet for whom the drama was a poetic form. His literary career was a response to the question of what it meant to be a writer, specifically a poet, in nineteenth-century America, and he is best approached as an American writer who responded to the same conditions as did the major writers.

The purpose of the present study, the first thorough study of Boker in more than fifty years, is to examine Boker within the context of American literary history, and the first chapter, while reviewing the general outline of Boker's career, discusses his theory of literature, paying particular attention to his understanding of the relationship between himself and his audience. In his works, as in his concept of his role as a writer, Boker was most concerned with the relationship between the individual and society. Thematically, then, his works treat a concern central to both American literature and American culture. Boker's most important works are his plays, especially the tragedies, written between 1848 and 1853, and the significance of these plays lies in their treatment of theme and character, both of which escape the limitations of the theatrical conventions Boker adopted. Chapter 2 examines three tragedies and four comedies written during these years; chapter 3 examines *Francesca da Rimini,* which was written in 1853, first produced in 1855, and published in 1856.

Influenced by Bradley's interpretation in *George Henry Boker, Poet and Patriot* of Boker as a sensitive genius crushed by the neglect of an indifferent and shallow society, recent critics have followed Bradley in reading Boker's plays as portrayals of innocent and noble individuals crushed by corrupt societies. Had Boker's plays done no more than present a simple conflict between noble individuals and corrupt worlds, they would be melodramatic rather than tragic. Although his plays do not boast the emotional force of great tragedies, the thematic complexity of his best plays surpasses that of melodrama. Instead of a conflict between a good individual and a corrupt society, such plays as *Anne Boleyn, Leonor de Guzman,* and *Francesca da Rimini* portray individuals who, frustrated by their social identities, are for valid reasons unable or unwilling to break free. These tragedies confront the paradoxes of human experience by placing the individual in a situation from which no escape is possible and for which no solution is satisfactory. In a nation founded in part on the assumption that the individual can break with his or her society and former life, Boker belongs among those writers who suggest that, if it is possible at all, such a break is fraught with difficulty and ambiguity.

One problem that kept Boker from achieving all he otherwise might was his inability to control his themes and thus create a fully unified work. This problem accounts for the failure of *Francesca da Rimini,* an ambitious play that never works out its themes as consistently as do *Anne Boleyn* and *Leonor de Guzman.* A second problem was Boker's inability to resist the temptation away from tragedy and toward melodrama, and this inability accounts for the failure of his last three plays, *Königsmark, Nydia,* and *Glaucus.* Consequently, chapter 4 devotes little attention to them. Similarly, the two books of poetry, *Poems of the War* and *The Book of the Dead,* that followed *Francesca da Rimini* are disappointing. Indeed, there would be little to recommend Boker's career after *Francesca da Rimini* were it not for his *Sonnets: A Sequence on Profane Love.*

These 313 sonnets, unknown until Bradley discovered and published them earlier in this century, form a significant, if uneven, work. As a love sequence influenced by the Elizabethan sequences, the work is a forerunner to the works of such poets as Edna St. Vincent Millay. As an examination of the individual's relationship with conventional society, the sequence continues the central theme of Boker's earlier plays. Unlike those plays, however, the subject of Boker's sequence came not from the remote regions of history, but from his own experience.

In his discussion of the autobiographical significance of the sequence Bradley concentrates on Boker's external biography, identifying the most important of the women addressed, for example, as Angie King Hicks. Material that has become available since Bradley's work does not affect that identification, but it does show that Boker's love affairs were more numerous than Bradley suggests, and the present study attempts to sort through both the sequence itself as well as Boker's earlier love sonnets in terms of their relationship to the "facts" of Boker's life.

Of greater importance is the relationship of the sonnets to Boker's internal biography. Boker began his career with the hope of becoming an important literary figure. By 1857, the time of the first sonnets to Mrs. Hicks, he recognized that his ambition would never be realized, and that recognition grew during the fourteen years covered by the sonnets to her. For Boker, the failure to fulfill his ambition was not so much a matter of his failure to write great works as of his failure to achieve recognition from the public. The sonnets spring from that need for recognition and return us to an examination of Boker's relationship with his audience.

During the first four chapters this study argues that four of Boker's works—*Anne Boleyn, Leonor de Guzman, Francesca da Rimini,* and the *Sequence on Profane Love*—have considerable merit; that *The Betrothal* and *The Widow's Marriage*—two of Boker's comedies—and the early poems on the nature of poetry, while of less intrinsic worth, are nonetheless interesting and competent works; and that the remaining plays and poems have little to recommend them. On the whole, Boker is intriguing and significant enough to command attention and respect, yet he remains a minor writer whose strengths never balance his weaknesses. As Boker himself realized, he failed to fulfill the promise evident in his best works. The fifth chapter assesses the nature of that failure.

Like other writers in the nineteenth century, Boker emphasized the importance of genius, which for him, as for others, was the ability of the imagination to perceive the essence of a given situation. Boker's failure was a failure of the imagination, and that failure is found in both his works and his literary theory. Capable of seeing that the relationship between the individual and society was complex, his imagination was not equal to the task of embodying that complexity in a sustained and satisfying literary work, and, at least in part, this failure resulted from his inability to develop a literary method adequate to his intentions. Boker's definition of literature was, from a theoretical point of view, mistaken, and a central element in that mistaken theory was his understanding of his relationship with the world around him. The reality of being a writer in nineteenth-century America was more complex than Boker's imagination allowed him to see; and while not historically important in the sense that he or his works influenced later writers, Boker is historically important for the light he sheds on the complex fate of the writer in America.

Oliver H. Evans

Acknowledgments

I am grateful for permission to quote the following: material from Boker's letters to Richard Henry Stoddard, published with the permission of Princeton University Library; material from the Boker-Taylor correspondence and from Boker's letters to John Seely Hart, published with the permission of Cornell University Library; material from Boker's *Sonnets: A Sequence on Profane Love,* used with the permission of the University of Pennsylvania Press; material from Edna St. Vincent Millay's *Collected Poems,* Harper & Row, copyright 1917, 1923, 1945, 1951 by Edna St. Vincent Millay and Norma Millay Ellis, used with the permission of Norma Millay Ellis. Parts of the third and fifth chapters originally appeared in *Educational Theatre Journal,* © 1978 University and College Theatre Association of the American Theatre Association, vol. 30, no. 2, May 1978.

Grateful acknowledgment is made to the American Philosophical Society for a grant that assisted in the research for this project. When I began the project, I was on the faculty of South Dakota State University, and I am grateful to that university for its assistance in the form of a grant and leave of absence. Similarly, I am grateful to Creighton University for its support of this project in the form of a Faculty Summer Research Fellowship.

During my work on this project the staffs at several libraries proved invaluable, and my thanks go to Cynthia McClelland and Jean F. Preston of Princeton University Library; Joan H. Winterkorn and Kathleen Jacklin of Cornell University Library; Neda Westlake of the University of Pennsylvania Library; and James G. Mundy, Jr., Librarian of the Union League of Philadelphia. My thanks are also due the staffs of Inter-Library Loan at both South Dakota State University and Creighton University for securing sometimes obscure material. A special thanks is due Leon Raney, Dean of the Library, South Dakota State University, not only for his assistance in locating material, but also for his interest in, and support of, this project.

I am also grateful for the support this project received from Professors J. W. Yarbrough of South Dakota State University, James Karabatsos and Reloy Garcia of Creighton University, and William Stafford and Darrel Abel of Purdue University. My debt to Professors Stafford and Abel extends back to the time I was a graduate student at Purdue. Since then, both have continued to encourage and support my projects, and both remain models for me of what the scholar-critic should be. I hope the present work comes close to satisfying their expectations.

Anyone who studies Boker is immediately indebted to the work of Edward Sculley Bradley, and that my assessment of Boker differs from Bradley's does not lessen that debt. Bradley's critical and scholarly works on Boker are a foundation for further studies of Boker; and had Bradley's editions of Boker's works not made those works readily available, the present study would have been both more difficult and relatively pointless.

Finally, I am fortunate that my wife, Eileen B. Evans, is also my colleague and that she brought not only her patience to this project, but also her knowledge of American literature. She has sat patiently through lectures on Boker and has read and reread sections of this book. Her comments and criticisms have improved the book; her patient support of the project has made studying Boker a pleasure.

Chronology

1823 George Henry Boker born October 6, Philadelphia, Pennsylvania.

1830–1838 Attends private schools, including Edge Hill School where he forms friendship with the school's owner, John Seely Hart.

1838 Father named manager of Girard Bank.

1842 Graduates from Princeton. Publishes "Norse Poetry" and "Odin" in *The Nassau Monthly.*

1843 "Pre-eminence of the Man of Letters" in *The Nassau Monthly.*

1844 Marries Julia Riggs.

1845 First child, George, only child to survive to adulthood, born.

1848 First book of poems, *The Lesson of Life and Other Poems,* and first tragedy, *Calaynos.*

1849 January 19, begins correspondence with Bayard Taylor. January, begins *Anne Boleyn.* May 10, *Calaynos* produced without Boker's knowledge at Sadler's Wells Theatre, London.

1850 *Anne Boleyn.* Writes *The Betrothal,* which opens in Philadelphia on September 25. By December 21, completes *The World a Mask.*

1851 January 21, *Calaynos* opens in Philadelphia. April 21, *The World a Mask* opens in Philadelphia. May, suffers first attack of a painful eye ailment that recurs throughout his life. By December 12, completes *The Podesta's Daughter and Other Poems.* December, first record of a love affair.

1852 *The Podesta's Daughter.* By September 1, completes *The Widow's Marriage.* October, record of a second affair. By November 14, completes *Leonor de Guzman.*

1853 January 31, writes Robert Montgomery Bird concerning the need for a Dramatic Authors' Bill and begins working to secure its passage. March 1–21, writes *Francesca da Rimini.* Writes *The Bankrupt.* October 3, *Leonor de Guzman* opens in Philadelphia.

1855 February, begins *Königsmark.* September 26, *Francesca da Rimini* opens in New York; opens October 10 in Philadelphia. December 3, *The Bankrupt* opens in New York.

1856 *Plays and Poems.* February, record of an affair with a married woman, perhaps Angie King Hicks. August 13, Dramatic Authors' Bill passes Congress.

1857 April, completes manuscript of *Königsmark, The Legend of the Hounds and Other Poems.* Begins writing sonnets that will become *Sonnets: A Sequence on Profane Love.* Last week of December, Boker's mother dies.

1858 February 8, Boker's father dies. Lawsuit with Girard Bank begins.

1859–1860 Writes *The Book of the Dead.*

1861 July, meets President Lincoln. September 7, writes "Upon the Hill before Centreville," first of his war poems. Throughout 1861–64 writes war poetry.

1862 November, with Judge John Hare founds the Union League of Philadelphia. Serves as its secretary, 1863–71.

1864 *The Will of the People,* a pamphlet arguing for Lincoln's re-election. *Poems of the War.*

1869   *Königsmark, The Legend of the Hounds and Other Poems.*

1870   President of the Philadelphia Club.

1871–1875   Minister to Turkey. December 30, 1871, writes last of sonnets to Angie King Hicks.

1873   Lawsuit with the Girard Bank settled.

1875   Envoy Extraordinary and Minister Plenipotentiary to Russia.

1877   June 23–July 9, writes fourteen sonnets (the second group of sonnets in the *Sequence on Profane Love*) that treat a brief affair in Paris.

1878   February, leaves diplomatic service and returns to the United States.

1879–1884   President of the Union League.

1880   Receives the gold medal of the Union League.

1881–1887   Writes the eighteen sonnets that form the third group of the *Sequence on Profane Love.* Last record of a love affair.

1882   September 14, Lawrence Barrett, playing the role of Lanciotto, revives *Francesca da Rimini* in New York to great acclaim. Elected to the Authors Club. Publishes *The Book of the Dead.*

1884   Elected to the American Philosophical Society.

1885   Writes *Nydia.*

1885–1886   Writes *Glaucus.* In 1886, begins work on an edition of his complete works; illness interrupts the project.

1889   November, confined to bed.

1890   January 2, dies.

1929   *Sonnets: A Sequence on Profane Love. Nydia.*

1940   *The World a Mask, The Bankrupt,* and *Glaucus.*

Chapter One

Boker's Career and Literary Theory

When in 1869 he sent Charles Warren Stoddard a copy of *Königsmark, The Legend of the Hounds, and Other Poems,* George Henry Boker wrote, "I trust . . . that you will like it far better than I do; for to confess the truth to you in confidence, I am no great admirer of the poems of one Geo. H. Boker. If all the world were of my mind, he would be a sadly neglected poet."[1] Boker was speaking ironically, for by 1869 he was not only "sadly neglected," but also bitterly disappointed by the failure of his plays and poems to excite the attention he felt they deserved and thereby to win for him the fame he desired. While a student at Princeton, Boker had decided to become a writer and between 1848 and 1856 had actively pursued a literary career. Although he continued to write during the 1860's— indeed he wrote until late in his life—Boker knew by 1869 that he had failed in his ambition of becoming a major writer. His career is the record of that failure.

To understand Boker's career, it is necessary to understand what Boker thought it meant to be a poet. Like other nineteenth-century American writers, he confronted the problem of writing in a country that had little use for literary pursuits and, like other writers, he had to demonstrate that the poet was important to society. Moreover, since America had little in the way of a literary tradition, Boker had to decide both what material literature should treat and the method literature should use to treat it.

In nineteenth-century America the issues of the poet's relationship with society, of his material, and of his poetic method often took the form of specific questions: Should a writer try to improve human life and, if so, how should he do this? Should a writer write for everyone or for a select group of readers? Should

a writer look for critical and popular acceptance in his time?
Should a writer treat "American" subjects? Should a writer use
existing literary forms, or should he devise new forms? Except
for the matter of American subjects, these questions were not
unique to American writers. But such questions had a particular
urgency for American writers. Whether a writer wished to or
not, he was forced to develop some theory that explained what
he was doing and why.

While Boker did not write systematically on literary theory,
he did treat the nature of literature in some of his college essays,
some of his poems, and occasionally in his letters. From these
sources it is possible to develop a statement of his theory. That
theory was not strikingly original nor entirely fortunate, and
he was himself unaware of some of the problems inherent in
it. But the purpose here is not so much to criticize Boker's
theory as to understand it and to see how he sought to fulfill
that theory in his works. To understand Boker's theory is, in
short, to understand why in the period of American literature
that saw the publication of *Representative Men, The Scarlet Letter,
Moby Dick, Walden,* and *Leaves of Grass,* an American writer
wrote *Francesca da Rimini.*

Youth: 1823–42

Charles Boker was already a successful Philadelphia businessman when his son George was born on October 6, 1823.[2] A
resident of Walnut Street, then in Philadelphia's best neighbor-
hood, Charles Boker was well known among other businessmen
for his shrewdness and ability. During the panic of 1837 Boker
enhanced his reputation not simply by surviving the panic, but
by improving his position at a time when most people were
losing everything. In 1842 he was named manager, and later
president, of the Girard Bank. Established as a national bank
in 1791 and purchased in 1812 by Stephen Girard, the bank
had barely survived the panic and was on the verge of collapse.
Through Boker's efforts, the bank survived, and he remained
its president until his death in 1858. Thanks to Charles Boker's
business acumen, the Boker family was wealthy and prominent,
and George Boker remained financially and socially secure
throughout his life.

Befitting the son of an important man, Boker's education began with private tutors when he was about seven and continued in 1831 at a school kept by Sears C. Walker, a Harvard graduate whose interest in astronomy led to his "Researches Concerning the Periodical Meteors of August and November" (1843) and eventually to a position with the United States Naval Observatory in Washington. At Walker's school Boker established a lifelong friendship with Charles Godfrey Leland, the son of Charles Boker's business partner and later famous as the author of *Hans Breitmann Ballads.*

In addition to Walker's school, Boker also attended John Seely Hart's Edge Hill School. By far the most influential of Boker's early teachers, Hart was thirteen years older than Boker and a graduate of both Princeton University and Princeton Theological Seminary. Remembered today as the editor of *Sartain's Magazine* at the time Poe submitted "The Bells" and as the originator of the first college course in American literature, Hart was an indefatigable writer of textbooks on education and rhetoric as well as the editor of an anthology of American literature. Late in his life Hart became Professor of Rhetoric at Princeton and while there wrote a life of Shakespeare for the Avon edition of Shakespeare's works.

Whatever Boker learned from Hart, more important was his attachment to his teacher, which lasted until Hart's death in 1877. Boker's love for Hart, whom he referred to years later as his "Dear Father Hart," stemmed from Hart's treatment when Boker, homesick and miserable, ran away from Edge Hill only to be returned by his mother. Expecting that Hart would inflict a severe punishment, Boker discovered instead that Hart was more concerned lest Boker had found something "disagreeable" at Edge Hill. "Thenceforth," Boker wrote Hart, "wretched and homesick as I was at times, I stayed firmly at Edge Hill through mere love of you; nor have the many years which have passed obliterated one incident of that occasion, nor lost you one corner of the heart which you then won."[3]

Following his early schooling, Boker entered Princeton in 1838. Then the College of New Jersey, Princeton was a conservative school with strong ties to the Presbyterian Church. But while Boker may have found Princeton's conservatism confining, he regarded that conservatism neither as something over which to agonize nor as something against which openly to rebel. At Princeton he lived a gentleman's life and impressed his classmates with the style in which he furnished his rooms. Moreover, as Charles Godfrey Leland says, Boker was "familiar, in a refined and gentlemanly way, with all the dissipation of Philadelphia and New York."[4] As in his later life, Boker moved easily in both the conventional and "dissipated" worlds, managing to play the conventional role expected of him while living a private life known only to his closest friends. He passed his classes without having to struggle, certainly without having to appear intellectual; and he was renowned for his ability to smoke a pipe and, at least to some extent, for his ability to write.

Boker's interest in writing found its outlet in the student literary magazine, *The Nassau Monthly.* Signing his works, E.J.R., E.I.R., Harry, Froda, and Novalis, Boker contributed eight poems and five articles between February 1842 and September 1843. Of the poems, the earliest three—titled "The Stranger Knight," "Childe Bertrand—A Ballad," and "Poetry—A Tale"—reflect his interest in the remote and exotic. Three poems are sonnets, a form Boker mastered, and the remaining two are translations from Old English. Boker's interest in Old English included an interest in Nordic mythology, and two of his essays are titled "Norse Poetry" and "Odin." In addition, he wrote essays on Carlyle's *Sartor Resartus* and Spenser's *Faerie Queene.*

Boker's most important college essay, however, is his defense of literature, "Pre-eminence of the Man of Letters." The essay was originally to have been an address delivered by Boker at his graduation in 1842. But having announced that Boker would make the speech, the faculty suddenly withdrew the honor when James Alexander, Professor of Belles Lettres, claimed that Boker's writings betrayed the influence of Hegel and were therefore corrupt. The charge was without foundation, and Albert Dod, a professor of mathematics, tried to change Alexander's mind, but to no avail. As a result, Boker did not deliver an address at his graduation. In fact, he did not attend his graduation at all. In 1875, when he recounted the experience to Hart, Boker described it as the first of a long series of frustrations that plagued his life, a frustration that was not eased by the publication of the essay in 1843.[5]

If the circumstances surrounding the essay's publication were a source of frustration, so too were the circumstances that made it necessary for Boker to defend literature. By 1842 Boker had decided to become a professional writer, and for the first time in his life his private wishes conflicted with the conventional role expected of him. The son of a successful man was expected to pursue a useful career, and Boker's father had little patience with his son's interest in literature. Charles Boker was not alone, of course, in objecting to a literary career. Such an attitude was common in America, which had little use for a pursuit that could not make a person rich and did not seem to contribute to the public good.

America viewed the artist as a person unable to meet the ordinary demands of life, and this view was sometimes reinforced by artists themselves. Charles Brockden Brown said that the artist was fond of "the solitary pleasures of his garden"; and in his discussion of Brown Henry Theodore Tuckerman invoked a stereotyped view of the artist when he wrote that Brown "recoiled" from "the exigencies of practical life."[6] Any plea on the part of the artist for solitude in which to work was regarded, at best, as an admission of the artist's inability to function in the real world or, at worst, as a form of malingering. As Oliver Wendell Holmes warned, since being a poet was an "easy way of shirking all the civil and social and domestic duties," indulging such "intellectual opium eating" would lead to "a serious loss to the productive industry of the country."[7] And Leland, who like Boker encountered resistance to his decision to pursue a literary career, remarks in his *Memoirs* that he was admonished again and again to note the success of "enterprising youth" who were working in business and "acting like men."[8] A literary career, then, was an effeminate and useless undertaking, and a poet was regarded, in Boker's words, as "a dreamer in a world awake."[9]

Significantly, Boker does not argue in "Pre-eminence of the Man of Letters" that a literary career is better than a career in business. Boker's father did not insist that his son enter business, although that possibility was suggested. Charles Boker's greater concern was more fundamental—that his son assume a position of some responsibility in society. The family's fortune had been made, and Boker's father urged him to pursue a career in law or diplomacy, one that would be useful and responsible. Thus in his essay Boker argues that the artist is a useful and responsible member of society who, in order to carry out his responsibility, must be left alone.

To support his argument, Boker distinguishes the artist from three types of people: jugglers and dancing girls—people who excel because of some physical ability, scientists, and statesmen. Not surprisingly, Boker easily dismisses jugglers and dancing girls as insignificant. His point is that art is more than entertainment and that to admire art is to admire more than the artist's technical ability. The artist offers more than entertainment and technical display, both of which are ends in themselves and soon grow tiresome. Like the scientist and the statesman, the artist is concerned with the intellect and with the reforming of society.

For Boker, the artist is superior to the scientist because the intellectual content of art is more accessible than that of science. The scientist's knowledge is important to, and understood by, only a few. While the results of science may affect the well-being of many, few of them can trace the experiments and thinking that led to those results. Literature, on the other hand, is open to all, for "the stream of literature flows through every country"; and just as it knows no geographical boundaries, so too literature knows no barriers of social class, but forms instead "a great republic of letters."[10]

This "great republic" represents a reformed society better than any society in existence. Consequently, the artist is similar to the statesman, for both strive to improve man's condition. Like the artist, the statesman must have intellect, and his work has value for other people. But the roles and methods of the statesman and the artist are diametrical and follow logically from their different situations in the world. Because the statesman exists in the public, political world, he lacks time for reflection. "The bustle and excitement attendant on a political life, the rapidity with which statesmen are hurried from scene to scene, the world of cases and anxiety in which they exist, give but little time for the quiet restraint and calm thought which are necessary for the man of letters" (76). Since the artist requires the solitude the statesman lacks, for one individual to combine the roles of statesman and artist is impossible.

Moreover, as a public man involved in the world around him, the statesman directs his efforts toward "man's present existence." His concern is to change "men's actions" and their "physical world," and "the effects of [his] conduct are immediate" (76). The world is changed because of the statesman, and the changes he effects are quickly and clearly perceived. As a result, the world of the statesman seems to be one of action and hence more real than that of the artist.

But the range of the statesman's influence is limited. He cannot change the human heart, and the changes he makes in the physical world are "generally confined to the nation over which he rules" (76). The artist, however, is not concerned with changing the physical world; nor is he even directly interested in the world around him. This does not mean that the artist is indifferent to what Boker calls "the cries of the miserable victims of crime and oppression" (78). But whereas the statesman perceives these "cries" as the result of imperfect institutions imposed upon the individual, Boker belongs among those nineteenth-century thinkers who argue that the institutions are the effect, rather than the cause, of the human condition. Until the human heart is changed, changes in the external world offer only a temporary, and ultimately illusory, relief.

Seeking to bring lasting and universal changes, the artist "toils increasingly to elevate the condition of the human mind" (78). In so doing, the artist seeks to overcome the provinciality of national and social identities and to reveal the eternal nature of man. The artist is a philanthropist who writes not for his own fame and fortune, but for the betterment of his world. Although the situation may appear otherwise to some, art is intimately involved in the everyday world and, by seeking to make that world better, contributes to human progress. While the statesman appears the more forceful and active person— the person more involved in directing human events, the artist is in fact the force behind history, for the artist slowly "forms the character of the nation over which the statesmen preside" (77). For this reason the man of letters is preeminent; and "if there is one offence in a nation which we should willingly forgive, it is the undue pride and admiration of its great men" (75).

Boker's defense of the artist is conventional enough. Indeed,

some of his distinctions, particularly that between the artist and
the scientist, are not carefully worked out. While his idea that
the artist is the creator of society recalls Shelley's "Defense of
Poetry," Boker's essay lacks both the power and depth of Shelley's. Further, the attempt "to elevate the condition of the human
mind," while noble enough in theory, often meant in practice
that during his career Boker contributed to the nineteenth-century gift-books and magazines that equated elevating the human
mind with developing a taste for the "refined" and "genteel."
Earnest and full of high purpose, Boker's essay remains an under-
graduate exercise that is more significant for what it shows of
his attitude toward literature than for its insights into the nature
of literature and the literary artist.

In terms of Boker himself, the essay indicates the depth of
his commitment to writing. In some ways, Boker can appear
to have been simply a rich man whose leisure allowed him to
dabble in literature, but whose commitment to literature was
no more than that of a dilettante. Life was relatively easy for
Boker, and he took pains to make it look easy. As Leland writes,
Boker "trained himself from boyhood to self-restraint, calmness,
and the *nil admirari* air, which, as Dallas said, is 'the Corinthian
ornament of the gentleman.' "[11]

Boker's development of "the *nil admirari* air" reflects a shallowness inherent in his social class which he never entirely escaped. Boker shared with his class the notion that to be too
serious, at least in public, about such things as education or
writing was to be unrefined, and it is important to remember
that it was the serious, the exclusive, pursuit of literature that
Boker felt compelled to justify. The rich amateur of letters was
not uncommon among Boker's social class, and to many of his
contemporaries Boker himself seemed no more committed to
literature than were several other wealthy men and certainly
no more disappointed with his lack of success than were they
with theirs. Even Marie Taylor, Bayard Taylor's second wife,
wrote in her memoirs that Boker "seemed satisfied with the
fame" his work achieved.[12] In fact, however, Boker was not
satisfied, but deeply disappointed because, although he kept
the extent of his ambition hidden from all but his closest friends,
he had hoped not merely to be a writer, but to be a preeminent
writer.

Public Career: 1843–56

Only between 1843 and 1856 did Boker realistically harbor such a hope and work to achieve it. Confronted with his father's objection to his career, Boker sought to placate him by studying law, a pursuit he felt might leave him time for writing. But he had no interest in the law, and he stopped his study in 1844. In that year he married Julia Riggs, a member of a wealthy Washington family, and the couple settled on Walnut Street in a house given them by Boker's father. No longer pretending to study law, Boker for the next twelve years devoted himself to writing.

Boker's publications, 1848–56. He published his first book of poems, *The Lesson of Life,* in 1848. The book, which consists of a "Prelude," the title poem, and fifteen miscellaneous poems including five sonnets, excited little notice, although Bayard Taylor's review in *The New York Tribune* became the means for Boker and Taylor to meet and to form a relationship that was among the strongest Boker enjoyed with any other writer. Taylor was fast gaining a reputation through his travel books, and his *Views A-Foot* (1846) was immensely popular. A friend of Richard Henry Stoddard, with whom Boker also formed a close relationship, Taylor was one of the writers who clustered about Rufus Griswold, later notorious for his treatment of Edgar Allan Poe, and by the late 1840s Taylor was regarded as a promising American writer destined to become one of the great lights of American literature.

Following *The Lesson of Life,* Boker completed and published *Calaynos,* the first of his plays. The play opened in America in 1851. In 1850 Boker published his second play, *Anne Boleyn,* which was never produced. In the same year his first comedy, *The Betrothal,* was produced, followed by a second comedy, *The World a Mask,* in 1851. In 1852 he published a second book of poems, *The Podesta's Daughter,* and wrote *The Widow's Marriage,* a comedy that was never produced because no actress could be found to play the lead. *Leonor de Guzman,* a tragedy, opened in 1853, the same year in which Boker wrote *Francesca da Rimini* and *The Bankrupt,* both of which were produced in 1855. Finally, in 1856 he published what amounted to his collected works, the two-volume *Plays and Poems,* which, while not including all he had written, included everything Boker thought had merit.

Many of his poems were first printed in magazines, and at different times in his career Boker enjoyed a close relationship with such periodicals as *Graham's,* which Leland edited for a time, and *Lippincott's.* Although in 1865 Boker denied that he was the editor of *Lippincott's,* he nonetheless exercised a great deal of influence over what the magazine published. Earlier in his career he exercised a similar influence over *Sartain's.* Originally *The Union Magazine of Literature and Art,* this magazine, devoted to "the elevation of American art, and the cultivation of taste,"[13] began publication in 1847 in New York City. In 1849 John Sartain purchased it and moved it to Philadelphia, where publication continued until 1852. During its brief history in both New York and Philadelphia the magazine numbered Poe, Thoreau, Whitman, and Longfellow among its authors, and its editor between 1849 and 1851 was Boker's former teacher, John Seely Hart.

Boker contributed a number of short poems to *Sartain's* as well as a turgid philosophical poem, "The Song of the Earth." He also served with Reynell Coates and Joseph Chandler as a judge for *Sartain's* prize article contest, an undertaking that required the reading of some four hundred essays and stories. In addition, he was an unofficial editor of the magazine. As the letters to Hart written between 1849 and 1851 show, Boker had a voice in selecting the poetry *Sartain's* published. Unfortunately, judging by the letters that survive, Boker was not asked to assess the poems of now well-known poets, but he did read many submissions by such poets as Fanny Osgood and Edith May, and he advised Hart not only on whether to accept their poems, but also on how much to pay for them. In addition, he assisted his friends in getting their work published, once telling Bayard Taylor that if Stoddard wished a poem published in *Sartain's,* he should go through Boker rather than approach the magazine directly (LT, March 21, 1850). Finally, when his friends published books, Boker saw to it that *Sartain's* gave those books favorable reviews.

So, too, such magazines as *Sartain's* devoted some attention to Boker's books. In December 1848, while still *The Union Magazine,* the periodical favorably compared Boker's *Calaynos* with Longfellow's *The Spanish Student;* in January 1849, the reviewer singled out for special praise Boker's "The Spirit of Poesy," which had been published in *The Snowflake: A Holiday Gift for 1849.* Similarly, *Anne Boleyn* was favorably reviewed in March 1850. In 1851 Leland published a lengthy article on Boker's plays; and in February 1852, six months before *Sartain's* ceased publication, the reviewer of *The Podesta's Daughter* said of the title poem that he could "remember nothing in similar form of construction more exquisitely beautiful."[14]

Throughout the years 1843–56, then, Boker was doing those things professional writers must do: getting his own works before the public; forming friendships with writers, editors, and publishers; helping his friends to get published and to get good reviews; hoping that his friends would see to it that his works were noticed. Yet despite his efforts and the sometimes favorable attention his works received, Boker failed to achieve a great or lasting fame in his own time. Many writers, including some whom later generations regard as preeminent, have endured their contemporaries' neglect. But for Boker, contemporary fame was intimately connected with his idea of the preeminent man of letters, and the theme of fame, which Boker touches on in his college essay, is central to such early poems as "The Lesson of Life" and "The Spirit of Poesy."

The need for fame. Its portentous title notwithstanding, "The Lesson of Life" has little intrinsic merit, but its portrayal of the poet helps define Boker's conception of his place in the world. As in "Pre-eminence of the Man of Letters," Boker here describes the poet as an isolated figure, and he cites Keats as an example of a poet destroyed by negative criticism and neglect. Yet Boker feels confident he can escape such a fate, for he is

> fitter to abide
> Harsh usage, or the bitter, nipping blast
> Of cold neglect.[15]

Unlike some poets, he will resist the temptation to escape such neglect by trying to achieve contemporary fame, for that fame is bought at the cost of betraying one's art. To "pander to the present time" (26), which Boker felt the Restoration poets had done, results in an ephemeral popularity, and the poet who seeks such popularity is pitiable:

How sad to hear ambition's votary whine!
To see him stretch his feeble hands, and seek
To grasp the phantom o'er the yawning grave!
                                                    (25)

Being a poet is a sacred and difficult calling requiring courageous
determination in the face of the little encouragement the poet
can expect. Although the poet may appear a simple and isolated
man, he must recognize that he is an extraordinary person who
can expect his reward only from a future age.

"The Lesson of Life" strikes notes common among those poets
now referred to as "genteel." Such poets, Stoddard, Taylor,
and Boker among them, thought of poetry as a mistress and
of their service to her as a sacred duty. In their correspondence
all three spend much time urging one another on in pursuit
of the laurel crown. "Let us all make up our minds," Taylor
wrote, "to become sacrifices (burnt-offerings!) at the altar of
divinest poesy" (LB, May 19, 1849). And whenever these poets
felt they had written only for money or had achieved the wrong
kind of fame, they reacted as though they had defiled their
mistress. Taylor, for example, wrote a poem welcoming Jenny
Lind to this country, and she elected to sing it. Taylor, who
thought the poem bad and lamented that by writing it he had
"defiled the temple of divine Poetry," felt he had to pray to
poetry for forgiveness (LB, September 19, 1850).

Poetry, then, was a mistress one served with the ardor of a
courtly lover, and, as in courtly love, serving this demanding
mistress was in part a curse, a theme found in another of Boker's
early poems, "The Spirit of Poesy." Here, the narrator describes
overhearing a poet sing a hymn to poetry. In his hymn the
poet claims poetry is his only love, one for which he will sacrifice
everything:

Come, Poesy! I'll woo thee like a lover.
I ask not fame; but thee alone I seek;
Thou art thy own reward, exceeding price.
With thee I'll sit and smile at envy's sneer,
Smile at the galling love of pitying friends,
And kiss the wrinkled brow of jealousy:
So thou wilt bless me.[16]

Poetry alone is meaningful to the poet because he knows that his poetic ability makes him superior to other people:

> For thou the drooping soul of dross canst purge,
> And lift the Bard above the common herd
> That toil and traffic, till their mental eye
> Grow dull or blind, for want of brighter use.
>
> (19–20)

As in "The Lesson of Life," the poet in "The Spirit of Poesy" suffers neglect, but is nonetheless confident of a final reward in heaven. Yet the poem ends not with a description of the poet's triumph, but with the narrator's description of the pain he imagines the poet must experience in this world:

> I pictured him a home, and rank, and wealth,
> A gentle, loving wife, and children fair,
> Fame, and all else which man on earth desires;
> And over these I spread the curse of song,
> And withered them to nought! What mental pain—
> What sickness past all cure—what thirsting thoughts,
> That came, like beggars pale, relief to ask
> At the closed portals of eternity,
> Must he endure who framed that troubled song?
>
> (23–24)

In "The Ivory Carver," a poem published in *The Podesta's Daughter* and later included in *Plays and Poems,* Boker offers a final, summary treatment of the themes found in "Pre-eminence of the Man of Letters," "The Lesson of Life," and "The Spirit of Poesy." The ivory carver, who wishes to carve a Christ, is surrounded by a world that does not understand him. His wife, for one, would prefer he carve, if not some toy for the children or a sword-hilt, perhaps an elaborate goblet "Fit for the lips of a bearded man."[17] While he is busy doing the work of heaven, she wishes he would concentrate on this world and would be happy if he were to

> Carve . . . something of solid worth—
> Leave heaven to heaven, come, earth, to earth.

> Come that thy hearth-stone may glimmer bright,
> And thy children laugh in dancing light.
>
> (260)

The carver, however, refuses:

> I labor by day, I labor by night;
> The Master ordered, the work is right:
> Pray that He strengthen my feeble good;
> For much must be conquered, much withstood.
>
> (261)

The curse of being an artist is heavy, for first the carver's wife and then his two children die, and the artist is outraged by God's treatment of him and for a time leaves off his work:

> Are these the blessings which Thou hast stored
> For the faithful few?—From sons of men
> Choose me for Thy chiefest rebel, then!
> Thrice cursed be the murderous, cheating thought
> That led me blindly! The hand that wrought
> This ivory fraud, thrice curséd be;
> For it slew the hearts that lived for me!
>
> (265)

In one sense, the carver's wife and children do live, for they become the inspiration that allows him to complete his work. Once he completes the Christ, the carver is given not only a triumphant reception into heaven, but also recognition on earth. As the poem ends, three Vatican priests find the Christ, and as Anselm, one of the priests, tells the others, this simple carving will stand triumphant "When Pope, priests, church, and the creed ye teach, / Have passed, like the heathen dreams, away" (276).

But while Boker could portray artists whose fame came posthumously, he was not himself content with such deferred gratification. Nor was he alone in thinking a poet should enjoy some measure of fame while yet alive. In "American Authorship," an article that appeared in *Sartain's* in 1851, the poet Champion Bissell argued that the neglect of authors was a thing of the past. Bissell pointed specifically to the career of Thomas Chatterton, an eighteenth-century poet who died a miserable and neglected man and whose fate was one nineteenth-century poets were anxious to avoid. Fortunately, Bissell argued, an author no longer needed to fear, since the reading audience had grown so large that any author who prepared himself would be successful. While making the conventional argument that an author ought not cater to popular taste, Bissell also argued that authors ought not hold themselves aloof from the public. "He who would be the light of the future must seek also to shine in the present."[18] And to cap his argument, Bissell went so far as to say that public acceptance was a measure of a poet's genius. Thus if a poet were neglected, such neglect proved the inadequacy not of the public's taste, but of the poet's genius. "The complaints of neglected men," Bissell concluded, "need be heard no longer. No good authors starve."[19]

For Boker, as for Bissell, contemporary fame confirmed the poet's genius. Although Boker could write Taylor during the 1850s that he was beginning to regard the public with contempt and that he cared nothing for the public's acceptance or rejection of him, he could not sustain his ambition through years of relative neglect; and his failure to achieve the kind of fame he desired in part explains the shortness of his public literary career. As chapter 4 will show, Boker's concept of the poet as a supreme being who of necessity must suffer neglect and his concept of contemporary fame as confirmation of the poet's genius landed him in a dilemma which, had he been fully aware of it, he could not possibly have resolved. At this point, it is necessary to understand the kind of fame Boker desired.

What fame Boker did achieve came largely from the stage success of some of his plays. *Calaynos* was first produced in London and had a good run. Similarly, the comedies that were produced pleased their audiences, and in 1855 Boker wrote Taylor that *Francesca da Rimini* was earning five hundred dollars a night (LT, October 22, 1855). Although casting difficulties sometimes kept Boker's plays off the stage, most of them were produced, and his royalties, as Arthur Hobson Quinn has shown, were often substantial and were sustained over a number of years. As Quinn concludes, "it is hardly the American playwright but the American poet who has a right to complain of lack of appreciation."[20]

And that precisely was the nature of Boker's complaint. His

books did not sell; nor did they receive sufficient critical attention. "My theatrical success," he wrote Taylor, "I never valued.
I had not, nor have I, any ambition to be acknowledged as a
mere playwright. . . . If I could not be acknowledged as a
poet I had no further desire, and no further active concern in
literature" (LT, October 22, 1855). Both Boker and Taylor
regarded their popular success as the wrong kind of fame because that success did not carry with it a recognition of them
as poets. "I am known to the public," Taylor said, "not as a
poet, the only title I covet, but as one who succeeded in seeing
Europe with little money" (LB, April 4, 1852). Although he
wrote travel books and novels, Taylor regarded his poetry as
his most important work; and although he wrote plays and hoped
they would be produced, Boker did not choose the drama because he wished a career as a playwright. The drama was simply
a vehicle for his poetry, and the right kind of fame, that achieved
through the sales of his books and through critical acclaim for
his poetry, would confirm Boker's belief that he was a genius.

    Literary materials and methods.   The particular kinds of
plays Boker wrote in search of that fame followed from his
theory that the poet expresses eternal truths. While still at Princeton, Boker found a prototype of the poet in Odin. In his college
essay titled "Odin" he describes the Norse god as a leader
who "beheld his people gazing in every direction, seeking to
penetrate the dark cloud which surrounded them." Odin, Boker
felt, "was a poet, and loved nature with an ardour the poet
alone can feel, he was as a little child alone in the vast temple
of the universe, keenly awake to any impressions." As a result
of his sensitivity to nature, Odin discovered some, but not all
of the essential truth of life. Once he proclaimed that truth
to his people, their "spell of darkness was broken, light was
given them, and that light burst from the mind of the inspired
Odin."[21]

    As Boker understood him, Odin was an inspired man who
through his love of nature perceived a part of essential truth.
Odin perceived this truth through the imagination, which Boker
regarded as the ability—or more properly the gift—of seeing
into the heart of the world. When active, the imagination placed
a person in an abnormal state of heightened excitement, a state
Boker claimed to experience while writing *Francesca da Rimini*
(LS, March 3, 1853). Through the imagination, the poet, almost

as though he were dreaming, is able to leave the temporal and enter the eternal.

Boker did not regard Odin, however, as a complete representative of the poet. While he felt that the light Odin brought his people was preferable to the darkness they otherwise inhabited, that light "was but as a taper to the noonday sun" when compared with the true light of Christianity. Consequently, Boker excused Odin's religious thought on the grounds that it was the best Odin could be expected to have developed, given his place in history. "We should not, therefore, too hastily condemn this great man for receiving divine honours; we should look on him as a wild, untaught, child of nature, on whose astounded mind the fire of genius burst with a brilliancy which startled him, quite as forcibly as his people" (26–27).

For the modern poet, the situation was different. He ought not to be a "child of nature" and ought not to depend solely on the imagination. Left, as in dreams, to its own devices, the imagination runs riot and creates not only nonexistent but also improbable things. Even Shakespeare, Boker said, must not be regarded as "an inspired being, [but] only the most intellectually perfect of God's creatures. The process by which he gained knowledge was the same as with other men, but it was infinitely more rapid and more comprehensive."[22] Boker was not himself given to wild, visionary experiences. While writing *Francesca da Rimini,* he claimed only to have experienced a heightened excitement. For him, the poet was a "dreamer" in the sense that his imagination, controlled by "memory and judgment," moved beyond the restrictions of his own time and place and into the universal (LH, March 26, 1870). Thus the ivory carver stares at an inert lump of material and reads the essential meaning within it.

Holding that literature should express universal truth, Boker believed that that truth existed independently of a particular time or place. While this belief might have led him to conclude, as Whitman did in *Song of Myself,* that "there was never more inception than there is now," Boker concluded that the universal was better sought in the past than in the present. "True greatness," he said in "The Lesson of Life," "builds upon the roots of things, / Builds on the fundamental homely truths" (63); and to arrive at these truths, the ivory carver looks to "the visionary past" (262).

Similarly, in "Countess Laura," another of his poems on the
nature of art, Boker portrayed the necessity of the artist's escaping the present. Carlo, the artist in the poem, deeply loves the
Countess Laura, who has died a year after marrying Count Fer-
nando. In response to Laura's death, Carlo struggles to capture
her essence in a portrait, and Boker's description of Carlo at
work recalls his earlier description of the ivory carver:

> And as the veriest drudge, who plies his art
> Against his fancy, he addressed himself
> With stolid resolution to his task.
> Turning his vision on his memory,
> And shutting out the present, till the dead,
> The gilded pall, the lights, the pacing guard,
> And all the meaning of that solemn scene
> Became as nothing, and creative Art
> Resolved the whole to chaos, and reformed
> The elements according to her law.[23]

For Boker, an artist needed to escape the present not only
because the present is distracting, but also because it lacks the
materials for art. In his most famous statement on literary theory
Boker told Stoddard, "get out of your own age as much as
you can" (LS, January 7, 1850). Boker belongs, then, among
those American artists who found America void of artistic materials. In "Ad Criticum," a poem originally published in *Königsmark,* he criticizes Europe for demanding that American artists
treat American materials. In Europe the artist is surrounded
by the raw material of art, but the American artist is not:

> 'Tis well for you beyond the sea,
>   Where every toiling mattock delves
> Among the spoils of history,
>   To bid us work within ourselves.
> All bare of legendary lore
>   Our grandest regions stretch away;
> These are the pictured scenes, no more—
>   These are the scenery, not the play.[24]

For artistic material to move a writer, or a reader, the material
had to be surrounded by a halo of suggestiveness, what Boker

calls "legendary lore." American material lacked such suggestiveness. Nothing had happened in America—or at least nothing had happened that could be transformed into literature.

To find literary materials, Boker turned to history and legend. Given, for example, Agnes Strickland's account of Anne Boleyn or Dante's account of Francesca and Paolo, Boker was free to use his imagination to look beneath the surface for elements of eternal truth that he could portray in his plays. In practice, he sought to demonstrate the nature of human experience by showing why characters behaved as they did and the lessons this behavior could teach. This is not to say that at his best Boker was didactic in the unpopular sense of the word, but that he was following Aristotle's injunction that the playwright portray the essential nature of an action. That essential nature was perceived by the imagination, which was itself held in check by history. As Boker told William Gilmore Simms, he regarded historical drama as "art bounded and working within the limits of history."[25] History provided the events; by providing an interpretation of those events, the poet portrayed their essential meaning.

But if his imagination found its subject matter in history, the poet still needed a form in which to express his insights. For Emerson and Whitman, the poet's imagination found expression through a spontaneous utterance. The poet's insight created its own form, and to force his insight into a preestablished form did violence to the insight itself. "What I experience or portray," Whitman said, "shall go from my composition without a shred of my composition." The poet should express his insight without recourse to established modes of expression, which Whitman regarded as "the richest curtains."[26]

Whitman and Emerson looked on the established forms and techniques of poetry as barriers to, rather than means of, communication. While Boker held that the poet's expression should be clear and free of affectations, he did not regard established poetic practice either as a "curtain" between the poet and his audience or as an affectation. In his attitude toward poetic technique he was a neoclassicist and thus held two assumptions about the nature of literature that differed from those of writers like Emerson and Whitman.

First, Boker assumed that the poet's insight, which for him

was a poem's "thought," was separable from its expression. A
poet might have the "spark" of genius, but that spark could
not be expressed except through the conventional devices of
poetry. Boker's position was that of Mr. Churchill in Longfellow's *Kavanaugh,* who held that "art is the external expression
of our thoughts."[27] As a result, when Boker discerned some
genius in Charles Stoddard's poetry, he urged Stoddard to
"study English rhythms with all [his] might, critically and pro-
foundly," because without a knowledge of these rhythms Stoddard would be unable to express his genius.[28]

Second, Boker assumed that poetry is governed by rules
grounded in the essence of the language, and that poetic practices, therefore, were not the product of a particular historical
period. When Melville said that all previous literature "but mul-
tiplies the avenues to what remains to be said," he meant in
part that new poets strive for new methods of expression.[29] It
was a mistake, Melville thought, to assume that the modern
Shakespeare would come garbed in the language of the Elizabethans. When Boker, on the other hand, wished to express
something new, he sought his method in the works of previous
writers.

Modern readers influenced by Romantic poetic theory tend
to see a neoclassical theorist as a drudge who devises rules for
other drudges to follow, and some neoclassical theorists certainly
invite such disdain. But Boker did not think of himself as a
drudge. He thought his approach to poetry rational—indeed,
scientific. One could deduce from the works of older poets
rules that could be assumed to operate in any time and place.
As Erastus Everett said in his *A System of English Versification,*
a book Boker much admired, "the laws of our verse are just
as fixed, and may be as clearly laid down, . . . as are the laws
of our syntax."[30] In one of his letters to Charles Stoddard, Boker
echoed this view when he wrote that "the whole system of
versification" is "purely logical."[31] Since to be a poet required
genius and since genius could not be taught, simply knowing
the rules of poetry did not insure a person would be a poet;
not knowing the rules, however, insured that a person would
not.

Escaping from his own age by looking to the past both for
his inspiration and his technique, Boker hoped to fulfill the

literary ambitions he formed while at Princeton. But as noted before, the success of his published works did not meet his expectations. He published *Calaynos* with E. H. Butler, but soon felt that Butler did not support the book adequately. Consequently, he changed publishers and published *Anne Boleyn* and *The Podesta's Daughter* with A. Hart, another publisher who proved, from Boker's perspective, unsatisfactory. As Boker told Taylor, he was finding his publishers' lack of attention increasingly distressing and the experience of having to approach publishers humiliating (LT, October 22, 1855).

Through Taylor's efforts Boker secured a new publisher, Ticknor and Fields, in 1855; and this, the most prestigious house of the time, issued his *Plays and Poems* in 1856. Although he said he did not hope "for an extraordinary success" (LT, October 22, 1855), Boker worried more about the success of this book than about any of his earlier works. Describing it as "a last dash at the laurel" (LS, September 4, 1854), Boker said he had "a life's venture on the cast" (LS, January 21, 1856). He regarded the book as a summation of his career; and its fate would mark "the turning point of [his] life" (LT, October 22, 1855). "By this work," he told Taylor, "I stand or fall" (LT, February 7, 1856).

Private Career: 1857–78

Following the publication of *Plays and Poems*, Boker felt he had fallen. He complained to Stoddard that the book was hardly noticed and that such notices as the one in the *New York Times* failed to comment on anything other than the book's "bulk" (LS, December 7, 1856).[32] Similarly, if Boker saw the review of *Plays and Poems* in the *North American Review*, he must have been disappointed.[33] Although favorable, the review was barely a page long, and instead of treating Boker's works in detail, it merely complimented Boker and hoped he would not rest his reputation on this work alone. Ironically, the work that constituted for Boker the culmination of his years of writing was for the reviewer but a preliminary performance that suggested Boker might yet become an important writer.

Plays and Poems did mark the turning point in Boker's life. Reprinted in 1857, the work did not have a great success, and

after its failure to excite attention, Boker gave up his literary
career. As he later told Edmund Clarence Stedman, "the rewards
of the poet in America are so slow and remote that none but
the faithful persevere to the end."[34] By April of 1857 he had
completed the manuscript of *Königsmark, The Legend of the
Hounds, and Other Poems,* but he did not publish the book until
1869. Moreover, Boker had neither the desire nor the time
to undertake another play: he found that not only were his
hopes disappointed, but also the leisure in which to write was
gone. Events, both public and private, demanded his time, and
these events coupled with the lack of recognition ended his
literary ambitions. In 1858 Boker could no longer follow the
advice he had given Stoddard and escape his "own age."

The first event was his father's death in 1858. As President
of the Girard Bank, Charles Boker had saved the bank from
ruin. But after his death, the bank sued the estate, charging
that Boker had been guilty of fraud. George Boker was not
so much worried by the threat to the estate as he was outraged
by the attack on his father's reputation. As joint administrator
of the estate, Boker was deeply involved in legal proceedings,
especially between 1858 and 1863. The lawsuit, which was not
settled until 1873, took much of his time, and so did the Civil
War, a second major obstacle to continuing his career. A sup-
porter of the Union, Boker was drawn into public life and was
instrumental in forming the Philadelphia Union League, an association of influential Philadelphia gentlemen who supported Lincoln and the Union cause. One of the cofounders of the League,
Boker served as its secretary from 1863 through 1871.

Between 1858 and 1865 Boker did not entirely give up writing, but the writing he did was either a private outlet or a
public service. During the early years of the lawsuit he vented
his rage by writing *The Book of the Dead,* a series of poems
castigating his father's enemies. During the war he contributed
to the Union cause by writing war poetry for newspapers. Given
its private nature, *The Book of the Dead* was not published until
1882. Some of the war poems, on the other hand, were collected
and published in 1864 as *Poems of the War.* In addition, Boker
continued to write love sonnets, something he had written from
the early days of his career, and by 1887 had completed a sequence of more than three hundred poems. But by 1857 his

love sonnets dealt exclusively with his extramarital affairs, and this remarkable and important sequence remained unpublished until 1929.

Once the outcome of the lawsuit was assured and the Civil War had ended, Boker had been away from writing too long to return to it. Aside from his sonnets, his literary activity now consisted largely of aiding other writers. In some instances, he substantially helped Southern writers recover from the Civil War. Such a writer as Paul Hamilton Hayne, for example, was "poverty stricken beyond all conception" (LT, February 16, 1869), and Boker secured publication for Hayne's works even though he thought they had little merit. In other instances, Boker acted as a literary advisor, criticizing and encouraging writers like Charles Stoddard and, as with Hayne, using his influence to find them suitable forums for publication. But he did virtually nothing in terms of his own work. By 1865 ten years had passed since the production of *Francesca da Rimini,* and while Boker could help Hayne recover from the war, he himself could not quite recover.

Furthermore, by the early 1870s yet another event required Boker's time. After the Civil War he continued his political activity. He was still secretary of the Union League, and, thanks to his early support of Lincoln and a pro-Lincoln pamphlet, *The Will of the People* (1864), an important figure in Republican politics and eligible for a diplomatic appointment.

Even that appointment was not without its frustrations. In September, 1870 Boker urged Hart not to try to have him appointed minister to England because Pennsylvanians already served in Russia and Turkey. Further, as Boker told Hart, President Grant had promised Boker an appointment by the summer of 1870, and the summer had passed without the appointment materializing. "Grant," Boker wrote, "is in a fair way to become that which he once told me he despised, a politician; for he has taken the first step towards that calling by qualifying himself as a liar" (LH, September 13, 1870).

In 1871 Grant did fulfill his promise by naming Boker minister to Turkey. Boker had hoped for an appointment to Spain or England, and at first his disappointment at being sent to Turkey led him to consider rejecting the post. At the urging of friends, however, he accepted with the hope that he would some day be appointed elsewhere. That appointment came in 1875 when Boker was named envoy extraordinary and minister plenipotentiary to Russia. From all accounts, he enjoyed this appointment and was so successful a diplomat that when the Grant administration left office in 1876, the Czar requested that Boker be allowed to remain as envoy.[35] But with the election of Hayes, Boker lost his post and returned to the United States in 1878. Ironically, he had resisted a government appointment while a student at Princeton; now, when he found that he enjoyed diplomatic service and that he was successful at it, events worked against his continuing in it just as they had worked against his continuing to write.

Final Years: 1879–90

Irony was to play yet another part in Boker's life following his return to the United States. He had craved recognition between 1848 and 1856, and that recognition came at last in 1882 with Lawrence Barrett's highly successful revival of *Francesca da Rimini*. The sudden acclaim for his earlier play awakened Boker's confidence in his literary ability as well as his interest in writing, and led him to publish *The Book of the Dead*, which enjoyed some success not for its literary quality but for its subject matter. The success led to a reprinting of *Plays and Poems*, this time with Lippincott, who had also reprinted it in 1869, and this work too enjoyed better sales than Boker expected. Suddenly after years of frustration, it seemed to Boker that he might be able to return to literature and to achieve the fame he had sought.

Ironically, the fame came too late, and Boker's hopes were short-lived. He did not complete a new play, *Nydia*, until 1885, and like others of his plays, *Nydia* was never produced. Barrett, who would have produced and acted in it, wanted the title role, and so Boker wrote a second play, *Glaucus*, on the same material. This time, however, an argument over royalties kept it off the stage, and neither *Nydia* nor *Glaucus* was published until this century. Finally, in 1886 Boker tried to revise *Calaynos*, but nothing came of the attempt or, ultimately, of his sudden fame. He was sixty-two when he wrote *Glaucus*, and he wrote no substantial works between then and his death in 1890.

In 1855 Boker told Taylor that no one would ever know his intense frustration and disappointment over the failure of his literary career. But in 1877 he did express those feelings in a letter to Hart. He was angry at Princeton for never having honored his literary achievement; rightly or wrongly, he felt that the lack of encouragement, which Princeton's failure to recognize him symbolized, together with such demands as the lawsuit, had destroyed his career. People, he noted, might think him successful in comparison with other men, "but the success, such as it is, is nothing to me. I have gained that which I did not care to win, while my poor little beloved poetical crown has lain withering at my feet."[36]

The terms "my poor little beloved poetical crown" recall the hyperbole with which Boker, Taylor, and Stoddard wrote about their dedication to art, and to dismiss Boker's words as the sentimental gushings of a man destined, whatever the circumstances of his life, never to be a preeminent man of letters is easy enough. Yet the terms should not diminish an appreciation either of the depth of Boker's disappointment or the extent of his accomplishment. That Boker persevered at a literary career as long as he did testifies both to the seriousness with which he regarded the writing of literature and to the need he felt to write. As work after work brought him little recognition or encouragement, Boker continued to write and, in the case of his sonnet sequence, produced an important work when he had no hope of its being read. Whatever the limitations of his accomplishment, Boker remained one of the "faithful."

Chapter Two

The Early Plays

With the exception of three comedies and one melodrama, Boker's early plays are romantic tragedies—five-act, blank verse plays set in the distant past and exotic settings. The genre of romantic tragedy recommended itself to a writer like Boker for two reasons. First, the plays imitated those of Shakespeare in language, time, and setting, and thus at least appeared to be part of a great literary tradition. Second, since the plays provided spectacle, they were usually popular with audiences; and since they were full of passionate display that provided an opportunity for histrionics, they were popular with actors. From a literary point of view, this popularity with audiences and actors often proved a drawback. The genre of romantic tragedy required that each scene have at least one intensely dramatic moment, and romantic tragedies easily degenerated into nothing more than spectacle, becoming what Donald Clive Stuart calls "a series of thrills," poorly suited to the development of character or the examination of theme.[1]

Boker, however, sought to make his plays more than exciting spectacles. As a rule, his plays treat characters, sometimes lovers, whose desires or ambitions are thwarted by a corrupt social order. He tried to make his characters individuals rather than types and thereby to create complex and powerful personages like those in Shakespeare. In addition, he tried to make the thought of his plays profound and to clothe that thought in blank verse reminiscent of Shakespeare's.

Of course, no playwright, including Boker, achieved anything that closely resembles the profundity, the dramatic excitement, or the poetry of Shakespeare's plays. More often than not, Boker was unable to escape entirely the limitations and difficulties inherent in his chosen genre. In a successful romantic tragedy character development must keep pace with the action, and such development must not only give rise to the requisite dramatic moments but also make those moments build inevitably to the catastrophe. Too often Boker's characters become functions of the plot, with the result that consistency and subtlety of characterization are lost. Lacking consistent characters, Boker's plays, particularly in the final act, lose their thematic depth and unity; and his language, rather than achieving dignity, is merely archaic, artificial, and bombastic.

Despite these weaknesses, Boker's tragedies are better written and more interesting than many similar plays. Through much of a given play, the characters are complex and the action does arise from that complexity. And because Boker is able to create complex characters and to sustain their complexity with more than common skill, his plays explore a number of themes and have more depth than do many of the plays of his contemporaries. Moreover, Boker brings a perspective rare in American literature to his themes. Unlike other American romantic tragedies, Boker's plays do not treat the commoner-hero thwarted by a corrupt social order. While his heroes and heroines are destroyed by a corrupt social order, not only are they a part of that order but also they remain loyal to it even as it crushes them. Boker handles his central theme—the conflict between the individual and society—not by pitting a noble outsider against a corrupt order, but by examining the fates of those who are simultaneously inside and outside of the society to which they belong. Just as Boker himself remained a part of his social class even as it restricted him, so too his characters find themselves unwilling or unable to break free of those forces that hold, and finally, destroy them.

Calaynos

Boker completed and published *Calaynos* in 1848, and the play was produced without his knowledge the next year in London. Despite its good reviews there, the play was not produced in America until January 1851; and in February Boker wrote Bayard Taylor that while the play was successful, he now found it filled with "such forced conceits—such stilted bombast—such uneasy, lumbering, labouring masses of purile [*sic*] vacuities" that it no longer satisfied him (LT, February 10, 1851). Boker focuses his comments on both the play's language and its thought. Yet for all the weaknesses of its language, the thought is its more disappointing element. Like Boker's later plays, *Calaynos* is concerned with the conflict between the individual and society as well as the related theme of appearance and reality. Its failure results from Boker's inability to sustain and integrate these two themes.

The plot of *Calaynos* involves the betrayal of Calaynos by his friend Don Luis; the play traces Calaynos's discovery of his friend's treachery and hence of his own blindness. Calaynos, a wealthy man who has devoted his life to philosophy, lives with his wife Lady Alda in a palatial retreat far removed from the corrupt city of Seville. As the play opens, Calaynos must leave his retreat and go to Seville, ostensibly to perform a rite of allegiance. In fact, however, he is going there to help Don Luis, whom Calaynos believes has fallen victim to Seville's corruption. As young men, Calaynos and Don Luis had spent their time devising plans to improve mankind's condition; but while Don Luis could devise better plans than Calaynos, Don Luis has failed to realize them. Instead, his search for happiness has led him to gambling; and rather than being a victim of Seville's corruption, Don Luis is himself a villain who dupes Calaynos into paying his gambling debts. Then, invited to visit Calaynos's estate, Don Luis further betrays his friend by trying to seduce Lady Alda.

To carry out his plan, Don Luis arranges a midnight meeting with Lady Alda at which he tells her that Calaynos has Moorish blood and that Calaynos bought her from her father. Both claims are true. Calaynos does have some Moorish blood, something which makes him anathema to pure-blooded Spaniards; and since Calaynos did enter a business arrangement with Lady Alda's father, he can be said to have bought her. To his credit, in order to spare her pain, Calaynos never told his wife of his ancestry, and both Calaynos and Lady Alda's father acted from noble motives when the marriage was arranged. The news understandably shocks Lady Alda who, choosing to faint at this, the most inopportune moment of her life, is carried off to Seville. When, sick and dying, she returns to tell Calaynos the full story of her ruin, he rushes to Seville, kills Don Luis, and is himself killed.

Although Don Luis is the villain, the play's central conflict is not so much between him and Calaynos as it is between Calaynos and Oliver, Calaynos's secretary. Oliver recognizes Don Luis's corruption from the first and attempts to show Calaynos the truth. He, however, refuses to listen; and his failure to see beneath his friend's appearance is part of his larger inability to perceive reality. While Calaynos prides himself on his knowledge and perception, he is blind to the truth that most nearly affects him. He has devoted his life to discovering "the chiefest springs of happiness," which for him comes from "faith in Heaven, and love to all mankind."[2] He has what he calls a "predetermined trust in man" that sets him "above the common herd" of ordinary, suspicious mortals (55). But in searching for this truth, Calaynos has isolated himself, and he can cling to his faith in the worth of other human beings only so long as he is not around them. Paradoxically, his love of mankind cannot stand too much of the reality of mankind.

Throughout *Calaynos* Boker's major interest is his characters' perceptions of the nature of good and evil, and as in many of his plays, he uses two settings as a device with which to explore the theme. The first setting in *Calaynos,* Calaynos's estate, represents an attempt to create an ideal society. In his castle Calaynos and his secretary study philosophy while Lady Alda is supposed to aid the kingdom's poor. But life on the estate is sterile and dull, particularly for Lady Alda. Calaynos, much older than his wife, behaves toward her, as she says, "More like a father than a husband" (8); and having been told of Seville by her maid Martina, Lady Alda longs for the life it represents.

Seville, the other major setting, represents the glamorous and exciting life of the court, a life antithetical to that at Calaynos's estate. Martina claims that Calaynos dislikes Seville simply because he dislikes pleasure:

> to him the gay are butterflies,
> Flitting around a light of which they die.
> He looks on pleasure as a kind of sin;
> Calls pastime waste-time.
>
> (10)

But Calaynos understands the reality lying beneath the appearance of pleasure in Seville. As he says to Lady Alda, "Martina

told but half'' (4) the truth about Seville and ignored both
Seville's vice and poverty as well as the corruption of a court

> Where every step is on a quaking bog,
> Where men spend lives on hopes and promises,
> And pine on smiles, and starve on smooth-told lies.
>
> (5)

According to Calaynos, to live amid the glamour and excitement
of Seville would in the end make one corrupt and misanthropic.
The world of Calaynos's estate and the world of Seville represent two modes of life. The one is a "cold pastoral" that seeks
to create a life in which innocence, simplicity, and honest deal-
ings with others may flourish—a world in which appearance
and reality are one. The cost, however, is human feeling and
involvement; love is abstract, not individual, and the appearance
of happiness masks Lady Alda's loneliness. In the world of Seville
feeling and involvement flourish, but that world hides corruption and hypocrisy. Ironically, while Calaynos sees the reality
of Seville, he is unable to see the reality of his own situation
and thus lives in a world of illusion.

Even more than the ambiguous nature of Calaynos's goodness
and more than Calaynos's limited powers of perception, Boker
is interested in the ambiguous nature of Don Luis; and Don
Luis—at least for most of the play—is the most interesting, most
complex, and the best realized of the play's characters.

Because it treats a Moor betrayed by a man he trusts, *Calaynos*
recalls Shakespeare's *Othello,* and no doubt Don Luis's character
owes something to Iago. But to pursue this, or any other, similarity between Boker's play and Shakespeare's is useful only to
show that the similarity is more apparent than real. Unlike Iago,
Don Luis is not primarily interested in making his supposed
friend suffer. Indeed, Don Luis cares little whether or not his
actions hurt Calaynos. His real interests are, first, to have his
gambling debts paid and, second, to possess Lady Alda. Moreover, Don Luis is not, like Iago, a profound and disturbing
study of evil. Instead, he is the study of a man who, in order
to placate his conscience, must convince himself that he has
no conscience.

Thus throughout most of the play there is a distance between

what Don Luis thinks he is and what his words and actions
show him to be. When, for example, he first plans to dupe
Calaynos into paying the gambling debts, Don Luis seeks to
quiet his conscience by blaming his actions on fate and God:

> I was not formed for good;
> To what fate orders I must needs submit;
> The sin not mine, but His who framed me thus—
> Not in my will, but but in my nature lodged.
> Formed as I am, I have no choice of fate;
> But must achieve the purpose of my being.
>
> (27)

Don Luis's evil, however, is motivated not by an inherently
evil nature, but by nothing more complex than the need to
pay his debts. If anything, Don Luis, both here and later in
the play, is simply unable to resist temptation; and it is easier
for him to escape feeling guilty if he can convince himself that
he has no conscience. Similarly, when he decides to seduce
Lady Alda, Don Luis seeks to blame the lady herself for having
"killed the latest seeds of good" in him, and he bids such goodness farewell in a speech which shows that his hatred of Calaynos,
rather than being fated or innate, is itself a balm for his, Don
Luis's, conscience:

> Farewell, all gratitude, and friendship's trust!
> Come, smiling sin, and pour thy honeyed words
> On tongue and lips, but in my heart pour gall!—
> Come, thin-robed sin, that show'st thy loveliness,
> But hid'st thy wickedness and keen remorse!
> That I may win my love, and hate her lord—
> O, when had love a conscience or a fear!
>
> (52)

The line "That I may win her love, and hate her lord" shows
that Don Luis's hatred of Calaynos follows, rather than motivates, his decision to seduce Lady Alda. Thus if it is accurate
to describe Iago's evil as "motiveless," to see in him an evil
that can never be adequately explained, the same is not true
of Don Luis. Don Luis needs money and therefore betrays Calaynos; he desires Lady Alda and therefore betrays Calaynos again.

Moreover, while Don Luis fears to some extent that his evil plans may be detected, he is more concerned lest he feel "keen remorse"; and just as earlier he tried to escape guilt by attributing his actions to fate, so now he seeks to escape guilt by both blaming Lady Alda for her own seduction and convincing himself that he hates Calaynos.

In Don Luis, then, Boker has created a character whose "evil" is a foil to Calaynos's "goodness." Don Luis must struggle to make himself appear a paragon of evil just as Calaynos has struggled to seem a paragon of good, and both suffer from the pride of believing that they can divorce themselves from those impulses that run counter to their ambitions. Don Luis can assuage his conscience only by increasing the extent of his evil; he can seduce Lady Alda only by hating Calaynos. Calaynos, on the other hand, can convince himself that he loves mankind only by refusing to acknowledge the existence of evil. Of the two, Don Luis is the more perceptive since he at least recognizes the possibility of goodness whereas Calaynos denies the possibility of Don Luis's being corrupt. But both men seek to escape the complexity of human experience by imagining that either evil or goodness is the sum of existence. Don Luis must convince himself that he is inherently evil precisely because he is not; and if the appearance of goodness hides a flaw in Calaynos, the appearance of evil hides a conscience in Don Luis.

Once having set the character of Don Luis in motion, Boker is unable to sustain it throughout the play's five acts. After abducting Lady Alda at the end of act 4, Don Luis disappears until the final scene, in which he and Calaynos duel. When he reappears for this scene, his character has been simplified. Calaynos's Moorishness, which earlier had been nothing more for Don Luis than a weapon he could use against Lady Alda, becomes in the final scene so consuming a passion that nothing short of Calaynos's death will satisfy him. Similarly, the characters of Lady Alda and Calaynos change as the play nears its conclusion. The plot demands certain actions from the characters, and as the characters become puppets of those demands, the play loses its thematic unity.

Of the central characters, Lady Alda is the least interesting and well developed, since Boker never decides whether she is the innocent victim of Don Luis's plot or a victim of her own weakness. She begins the play "A lonely queen, without a court or friend" (5), and because of her inability to be as virtuous as Calaynos, whose "every wish and act inclines to good," she accuses herself of having a "wavering mind" (9). Soto, Don Luis's servant, underscores this aspect of Lady Alda's character, describing her to Don Luis as "weak, of fickle mind" and "thence easily led" (66).

But neither Lady Alda's nor Soto's words are borne out by her actions. When anyone criticizes Calaynos or seeks to turn her against him, Lady Alda is quick to defend him. When she discovers Don Luis loves her, her loyalty to Calaynos never wavers. Further, her being "easily led" to the interview with Don Luis is the result of Calaynos's having placed her in a situation she has no reason to suspect is dangerous, and her inability to see beneath Don Luis's appearance is the result of Calaynos's having allowed her no experience of the world. Throughout the first four acts, then, Lady Alda is a victim, rather than an agent, of the play's action; and at the moment of her greatest danger, the moment when she is required to act, she appropriately faints.

In her final scene (5.1), however, Lady Alda's character is changed. The plot now demands a dramatic scene in which she returns to Calaynos, is reconciled with him, and dies. Thus when Calaynos forgives Lady Alda for what in fact was not her fault, she replies:

> O god-like man! thy speech surpasses hope;
> I did not look for this from even thee;
> I only wished to crawl to thee and die:
> For I have shamed thee in the face of man.
> I've made thy name a sneer and mockery;
> And fools may spit their slander on thy fame,
> To gall thy pride, and shake thy glorious mind.
> O fie, O fie! that I should do this act—
> This act beneath pollution!
>
> (95)

Precisely what Lady Alda is responsible for having done is difficult to determine, and the guilt she confesses in this speech is undeserved. While her meeting with Don Luis was ill advised, she can hardly be held accountable for going to Seville since she was unconscious at the time; once there, she presumably had no control over her fate. Even were one to argue that Boker is using conventions of social behavior under which Lady Alda is guilty, or that Boker is portraying the not uncommon phenomenon of a person's feeling guilty for something that was not that person's fault, he fails to make either real, and Lady Alda, who claims "half the fault" for her "act beneath pollution," might have done better to place that fault on Calaynos.

Calaynos himself is the most serious weakness in the play, and this weakness lies not only in his obtuseness and the triviality of his philosophy, but also in Boker's failure to integrate Calaynos's Moorishness with the play's theme of appearance and reality. According to the Prologue, Calaynos's Moorishness is central to the play:

> Our plot turns on the loathing which they feel,
> Who draw their spotless race from proud Castile,
> For those whose lineage bears the faintest stain
> Of the hot blood which fires the Moorish vein.
> No time can reconcile, no deed abate,
> For that one taint, the haughty Spaniard's hate. . . .
> (vii-viii)

Technically, these lines are true, for the crisis occurs when Lady Alda learns of her husband's ancestry. But throughout the rest of the play, Boker encounters difficulties in handling Calaynos's Moorishness.

For one thing, it is necessary that no one in the play know of Calaynos's race until the right moment, and Boker handles this necessity clumsily. According to Soto, "half of Spain" knows of Calaynos's ancestry and that is why Calaynos refuses to let Lady Alda visit Seville (61). Yet Don Luis does not know what "half of Spain" knows, although, when Soto tells him of Calaynos's ancestry, he vaguely remembers having "heard it when a boy" (61). However, as young men Calaynos and Don Luis had devised plans for improving human life; thus apparently at that time Don Luis had forgotten what the Prologue claims "No time can reconcile, no deed abate."

Boker is similarly clumsy in his handling of Lady Alda's discovery of Calaynos's background. Early in the play she remarks that his ancestors, whose portraits hang in the castle, resemble Moors. But when, in order to convince her that Calaynos is a Moor, Don Luis points out that the name Calaynos is Moorish, Lady Alda lamely replies, "I never thought of that" (79). Although she has noticed that her husband's ancestors may be connected with the Moors, she has not noticed the relevance of his name.

More important than the clumsiness with which Boker handles the matter of Calaynos's race is his inability to tie it to the play's themes. If one adopts the Prologue as a guide to the play, *Calaynos* is meant to treat the theme of an inherently noble individual in conflict with a corrupt society that arbitrarily excludes him in the same way that "the sound man the loathsome leper shuns" (viii).[3] As a result, Calaynos's race should be interpreted as an artificial distinction his society imposes on him and that it then uses to justify destroying him. But since virtually no one knows of his ancestry until late in the play, that ancestry motivates little of the action. Don Luis swindles Calaynos and decides to abduct Lady Alda before he knows, or remembers, that Calaynos is a Moor. Martina, from whom Soto learns of Calaynos's race, dislikes Calaynos not because he is a Moor, but because he is an intellectual who regards her as frivolous. Even Calaynos himself does not seem unduly troubled by his race. Although he does not live in Seville, that is not so much caused by his being a Moor as by Seville's being corrupt; and Seville's hypocrisy, vice, and intrigue—the things Calaynos has sought to escape—have little to do with the city's racial attitudes. At no point, then, does Boker establish a clear relationship between Calaynos's race and the theme of the individual's conflict with society.

Nor does he establish any significant relationship between Calaynos's race and the theme of appearance and reality, although at one point he tries to suggest that Calaynos's race is the "one seed of sin" (99) Calaynos has not escaped by establishing a safe and uncorrupted life. But Calaynos's "sin" is not so much his race as it is his pride in his abilities both to perceive reality and to love his fellow man, neither of which he can do. Furthermore, Boker cannot have Calaynos's race function both as a meaningless convention his society uses against him and as a flaw in his character. To treat Calaynos as a victim of social convention forbids the use of Calaynos's race as a flaw in his character, since if his race is meant to be a "sin," his society is correct to judge him on that basis.

Boker makes no attempt to resolve the problems of Calaynos's race. Indeed, race amounts to little more than a device to effect, first, Lady Alda's fainting and, second, Calaynos's killing of Don Luis. In the end, Calaynos, not hitherto associated with revenge or cruelty, must kill Don Luis and be killed himself. Since Boker has only the fifth act in which to transform Calaynos from a man devoted to thought and love into an implacable avenger, he relies on his "hot blood." When Oliver asks if Don Luis shall go unpunished, Calaynos, looking at the portraits of his ancestors, says:

> No, No, by Heaven!
> Those fellows on the wall would haunt me then.
> I hear your voices, men of crime and blood,
> Ring in my ears, and I obey the call.
>
> (99)

Calaynos goes on to say that his sword "is thirsting for man's gore" because of his Moorish ancestry, that his "tiger spirit" is roused, and that a "bloody mist" clouds his vision (100). Now what had been a "mere taint" of Moorish blood entirely controls Calaynos and provides Boker with a means of motivating the play's final spectacle.

Although the character of Don Luis and the handling of the theme of appearance and reality are initially intriguing, little good can finally be said about *Calaynos*. The plot of the play is awkward; its themes confused; and its language, as the lines quoted in this discussion suggest, "uneasy, lumbering, labouring." Not a profound thinker himself, Boker fails to make Calaynos convincingly profound; nor is he able to settle on the type of play he wishes to write. The play, as Boker's first, shows how much he had yet to learn about writing plays. Fortunately, by the time he wrote *Anne Boleyn,* he had learned a great deal.

Anne Boleyn

Anne Boleyn deserves a greater reputation than it enjoys. It is, to be sure, not a successful stage play. Although the story of Anne Boleyn is itself dramatic, Boker's play relies heavily on soliloquies to characterize Anne, and the lengthy soliloquies do not make for exciting drama. But Boker does solve the problems of character and theme that marred *Calaynos.* In *Anne Boleyn* the characters are consistent and complex, and the action arises out of that complexity and moves inexorably to the catastrophe. And since action and character are perfectly joined, the play sustains its several themes.

Like *Calaynos, Anne Boleyn* treats the themes of pride, appearance and reality, and the individual in conflict with society. In addition, it touches on such themes as time, fate, and the role of the artist. Yet the mere number of themes is not as noteworthy as is the subtlety with which Boker probes them. In its handling of character and theme, then, *Anne Boleyn* is a more assured work than *Calaynos.*

Boker began writing *Anne Boleyn* in 1849, telling Bayard Taylor in January that he was "about to write another tragedy" and was, therefore, "wide awake" and unconcerned with the critics (LT, January 19, 1849). Later that month he told Hart, "Anne Bullen is driving on like fury, at the rate of one hundred lines a night. She comes out easier than Calaynos. . . . I would rather have female than male children, if they are all like her" (LH, January 30, 1849). In February, Boker again wrote Hart, this time saying that the second act was underway (LH, February n.d., 1849). According to a letter to Richard Stoddard, the finished work was to "go to press" by September 20 (LS, September 5, 1849). The play, with a Prologue in which Boker objects to critics who claim he can do no more than imitate Shakespeare, was published in 1850, reprinted without the Prologue in the *Plays and Poems,* but never produced.

Boker's source for *Anne Boleyn* was the fourth volume of Agnes Strickland's *Lives of the Queens of England* (1840–48). Although widely read in the nineteenth century, Strickland's work was more than a popularization of history. Strickland was a thorough scholar who examined the then-uncalendared State papers; and to do so, she had to challenge the policy that barred women from the room housing them.[4] From these papers Strickland quotes Anne's speeches during her arrest, trial, and before her execution; and Boker borrows heavily from these speeches, often doing little more than turning the prose into blank verse. But in providing Boker with the historical facts and Anne's speeches, Strickland provided only the historical boundary within which his imagination had to work. In writing his play, Boker had to create the speeches and to dramatize the events that led to Anne's dignified and heroic defense at her trial and execution. His imagination had to portray the characters and society that confronted Anne and to reveal the gradual development of her character.

Anne confronts a society that invents a trap to remove her from the throne. The legal case against her rests on the charge that she has been unfaithful to Henry and is thus guilty of treason. The charge of adultery, in turn, rests on the statements of Anne's groom, Mark Smeaton, and Lady Rochford, the wife of Anne's brother. Historically, Smeaton confessed under threat of torture and even at his death did not recant. Nonetheless, his story was probably fabricated, and Boker portrays him as a weak man whose bragging of his friendship with Anne makes him a pawn in the hands of her enemies. Lady Rochford, on the other hand, made her accusations, including the accusation that Anne and Rochford were guilty of incest, out of jealousy and malice. As Henry says of her, "If Hell were swept, to find its vilest soul, / That soul would blush at sight of this good lady" (160).

While the corruption of the society that destroys Anne is one of the play's major themes, Boker does not portray the corruption at Henry's court as all of one piece. Instead, the society that destroys Anne is composed of diverse forces, each with its special motives. Some of Anne's enemies, for example, plot against her because she is a woman; some because she is a Protestant; some simply because she has offended them. Jane Seymour, who attempts to imagine herself "the instrument of justest heaven" in unseating Anne, is in fact attracted by the glamour of being "a real annointed queen" (132), while Norfolk, Anne's uncle, is motivated by nothing save his lust for "power, power, power" (212).

To underscore the corruption of the court, Boker sets one of the scenes (2.4) in an area of London called "Safety" by the thieves who inhabit it. In terms of the action, the scene functions only as an occasion for the poet Thomas Wyatt, one of Anne's allies, to tell Rochford that Anne is in danger and should try to save herself. Thematically, setting the scene beyond "The utmost pale and influence of the court" (145) provides Boker with an opportunity of presenting the reality that lies beneath the court's civilized appearance, for Wyatt's description of Safety applies not so much to it as to the court:

> Here is a place as innocent of rule
> As the dun sands of savage Araby.
> Here pilferers divide their filchéd rags,
> And bolder robbers share their golden spoils;
> Here crime is native, natural, unabashed,
> Walking abroad in easy confidence;
> . . . .
> No law is here,
> Save what the dwellers make, and that is shifting.
> (143–44)

The center of the play's corrupt society is Henry, who wishes to rid himself of Anne to gratify a whim. Henry, however, is more than a scheming villain (and when the play was first published, his character excited the most controversy).[5] As Boker portrays him, Henry is, like Don Luis, a man whose principles are not strong enough to make him behave justly. He recognizes that he is the victim of his own power, that because he can do as he wishes, he has never learned to discipline himself:

> O, I would rather be
> The snarling cynic in his squalid tub,
> And master of myself, than England's king,
> Reared to indulgence of each flimsy whim
> That passion hints at. 'Tis the curse of kings,
> This slaving to our pampered appetites.
> (171)

He further recognizes that his love for Jane is nothing more than physical desire. When she is present, Henry is enthralled by "the hot thrill of her loveliness," but when she is absent, "this same fever, / That fiercely glowed erewhile, calms and is cooled" (167). The case is quite different with Anne. The mere thought of her brings Henry "a holy peace" (167).

Yet while he is not strong enough to behave justly, Henry must delude himself into believing that his conscience is clear of wrongdoing. Thus when he becomes convinced that adultery is the only charge that can be fabricated against Anne, Henry demands that Norfolk produce evidence enough "To force conviction to the very core / Of [Henry's] conscience" (159). Because of his need to feel free of guilt, Henry is easily manipulated by Norfolk—or anyone—who can assist him to his ends while simultaneously soothing his conscience. Indeed, the person with Henry at a given moment is likely to control him, a point that is graphically illustrated at the play's turning point (3.5).

As this scene opens, Anne, who has been trying for some time to talk with Henry, finds him alone. Her only hope of escaping her fate is for Henry to act honorably and, although at first he is enraged by her presence, he is soon in love with her once more and the two are reconciled. Feeling secure, Anne unwisely leaves Henry alone. Jane immediately enters and by the end of this scene has won Henry from what he calls "the witchery of sly Anne's tongue" (173).

Once Henry has committed himself to Jane—and Jane wisely does not leave him by himself—Anne's hope of surviving is gone. In the next scene (4.1) Henry openly accuses Anne of adultery. The accusation takes place at a tournament, and Boker's handling of the scene, particularly of Henry's motivation, is one of his major accomplishments in this play. Here Boker had to work with relatively slight historical material. According to the records, Henry suddenly left the tournament, Anne soon followed, and her friends Rochford and Norris were quickly arrested. But history is unclear as to precisely what happened at the tournament, and why. "The popular version," as Strickland says, held that Anne, "either by accident or design, dropped her handkerchief." When Norris, a participant in the tournament, retrieved it, he "presumptuously wiped his face with it" before returning the handkerchief to Anne. At this, "Henry changed colour, started from his seat, and retired in a transport of jealous fury."[6]

In Boker's play Anne, secure that she and Henry are again in love, dares to plead that the tournament be stopped so that neither Rochford nor Norris will be wounded. When Henry, who claims to believe that both men are Anne's lovers, refuses, Anne herself orders the herald to sound a retreat, an action that angers Henry. "In her terror," as the stage direction says, Anne drops her handkerchief; when Norris kisses and returns it, Henry calls Anne a "Shameless adulteress" and storms out (176). Thus Anne's actions are innocent, and her willingness to stop the tournament is motivated by her belief that her relationship with Henry is once more secure.

Boker's explanation of Henry's action in this scene is an even more masterful touch. Strickland speculates that "Henry, who was anxiously awaiting an opportunity for putting his long-meditated project against the queen into execution, eagerly availed himself of the first pretext."[7] But in Boker's play Henry does more than seize upon a "pretext" for accusing Anne. He also seizes this opportunity of insuring that his internal conflict can no longer affect his behavior toward Anne.

By publicly accusing Anne, Henry leaves himself no possibility of once more changing his mind about her. As he later says, the effect of his accusation at the tournament is to make the issue of Anne's adultery lie "between her and me, / And not between her innocence and guilt" (179). Henry cannot now allow Anne to escape conviction, for that would bring infamy upon himself and, since he and England are one, upon England. For the good of England's reputation, Anne must be convicted. Henry must now "prove [the] charge" against her, "or by conviction sure / Seem to attest it" (179).

Thus Henry equates his "flimsy whim" of being rid of Anne with the preservation of England's honor, and he leaves himself no room for private struggles with his conscience. England's well-being demands that a court convict Anne; and if a court convicts her, Henry will be unable to pardon her since the court's "candid verdict will stop pity's ears" (180). Moreover, at least as Henry sees it, if a court finds Anne guilty when in fact she is innocent, the court, not Henry, is guilty of her death.

As Henry says, "I escape stainless" (180). Henry has solved his internal conflict, then, by creating a situation that demands he act in a certain way and yet allows him to believe he is innocent, and Boker's portrayal of Henry's method of overcoming his conflict with his conscience is one of the playwright's most subtle pieces of characterization. In Henry's court there is indeed "No law, . . . / Save what the dwellers make, and that is shifting."

Anne's innocence is no match for the corruption of her society, and her earlier ability to manipulate events is no help in her struggle with Henry. Her enemies are too powerful to be outwitted; in pitting her against her society, Boker could not show her literally triumphing over the world around her. Instead, he shows Anne's figurative triumph, a triumph achieved through her nobility and courage as she confronts her fate.

To show this triumph, however, Boker faced the difficult problems not only of making Anne capable of nobility and courage, but also of making her someone with whom the audience could sympathize. The problem of creating sympathy for Anne arose because of the failures of her own past. As Strickland wrote, "no one who dispassionately reflects" on Anne's rise to power "can reconcile it either with her duty . . . or those feelings of feminine delicacy" that should have stopped her attempt to win Henry from Catherine.[8]

Although a modern audience may smile at, or be outraged by, the phrase "feelings of feminine delicacy," that audience must agree that early in her career Anne had little sense of morality, simple decency, or nobility. When she came to Henry's court in the 1520s and found herself pursued by Henry, she of course confronted a dangerous situation. Yet she seems to have been perfectly aware of her power over Henry and perfectly willing to use that power to gain her political aims. She secretly married Henry in January 1533 even though Henry's marriage to Catherine lasted until May, when Thomas Cranmer, the archbishop of Canterbury, usurped the power of the Pope and annulled the marriage. Catherine lived in isolation and misery until her death in 1536, and, according to some accounts, Anne publicly rejoiced on learning of Catherine's death. Ironically, Anne was executed a few months later. But as Bradley says, Anne's "sad fate loses some of its poignancy" when her earlier pride and her joy at Catherine's death are recalled.[9]

A measure of Boker's success in *Anne Boleyn* is that, despite these problems, he succeeds in creating sympathy for Anne. He does so, first, through his portrayal of Anne's gradual understanding of the essential nature of her earlier life. More clearly than any character except Wyatt, Anne sees both the corruption of her society and the meaninglessness such corruption gives the lives of those who practice it. He further creates sympathy by portraying Anne's increasing concern for Norris and Rochford who, while as innocent as she is, are caught up in the events that engulf her. And finally, Boker creats sympathy by portraying Anne's love for Henry, a love that, like her innocence, proves to be real.

When the play opens, Anne, adept at surviving in the world of intrigue, is at the height of her power and influence. In act 1, scene 3, however, she discovers that Henry's attitude toward her has changed. Angry at Anne for interrupting his conversation with Norfolk, Henry refuses either to help the German Protestants, which Anne asks him to do, or to defend Anne from Norfolk's insults. In her soliloquy that closes the scene Anne asserts that her "noon of power" (129) will not be undone by a baseless fear that the king has turned against her:

> Great souls are cheerful with their inborn power,
> Feeling themselves the rulers of events,
> The sinewy smoothers of the roughest times,
> And not the slaves of outward influence.
>
> (129)

Thus Anne devises a scheme to win Henry back. Once she can find him alone, she will pretend to be angry with him and then seem to forgive him "at one great eager gasp" (130). Through this "seeming noxious wrath," Anne plans to "puzzle all [Henry's] wits" and to achieve "a new-born love of double power" (130).

Anne seeks an opportunity to carry out her plan in the first scene of act 2. But instead of finding Henry alone, she discovers him with Jane. Until now Anne has thought "Some state affairs" had "galled the fretful edge / Of hasty Harry's rash but loving heart" (130). Seeing Henry with Jane, Anne recognizes more

fully the extent and nature of Henry's change, and the shock
of this discovery causes her to react violently, a reaction that
marks the low point in her development.

At first, Anne says that her fall is a trial imposed by heaven.
Later in the play she will see that her fall is in part a test of
her strength and in part a punishment for the suffering she
inflicted on Cardinal Wolsey and Catherine, and she will be
able to accept it as such. At the beginning, however, her submission to heaven is feigned and extreme:

> Kind Heaven, have mercy on my feebleness!
> If this be trial of my strength, I yield;
> I do confess my utter helplessness;
> I bow me prostrate, a poor nerveless woman—
> A queen no more. I'll trample on my pride,
> And follow meekly where thy finger points.
>
> (136)

In spite of these words, Anne does not in fact believe her
fall the work of heaven. Hers "is a grievous wrong, / By man
inflicted" (136). Hence she seeks revenge by cursing Jane and
any child—the future Edward VI—born to her and Henry. Losing her power to control events directly, Anne must now try
to control them indirectly, through a curse:

> If to these murderers of my heart's dear peace
> A child be born, may she, in that sweet time
> When infant babble opes all heaven to her,
> Feel the cold hand of death draw, day by day,
> The clinging spirit from her! May her child
> Live in the vexings of a troubled time,
> And, issueless, die young!
>
> (137)

Significantly, however, Anne stops short of cursing Henry:

> May he—O God
> I cannot bid a curse light on the head
> Of him my child calls father!
>
> (137)

Although she has used her sexuality as a means to the throne and although she has said she will use it again to regain her control over Henry, Anne's inability to curse him indicates that her love for him is more than sexual.

Anne's love for Henry accounts for two of her later actions. It explains, first, why she will support no plan to free her that endangers Henry or constitutes treason against him. When just before her execution Anne learns of Wyatt's plan to raise a rebellion among the common people, she not only refuses to listen to it, but also says she will tell Henry of any plan that involves treason and danger to "the safety of his majesty" (227). She is, then, loyal to Henry and through him to the society that crushes her, and is both unwilling and unable to free herself if her freedom involves treason. Tragically, Anne is caught between two noble emotions: her desire to vindicate and save herself and her desire to love and remain loyal to Henry.

Second, Anne's love for Henry explains her actions at the turning point in the play (3.5). When she first saw that Henry's attitude toward her had changed, Anne had said she would use deceit to regain her power over him. But when she meets Henry in this scene and he accuses her of being proud, she does not react angrily so that she can pretend to forgive him. Instead, she confesses her pride, and her speeches in this scene have a dignity and restraint not found in her soliloquy at the end of act 1 or in her curse of Jane and Edward:

> I have sinned,
> And tried the mercy of indulgent Heaven
> Beyond all bounds that human reason knows.
> I have been arrogant, to judge my kind
> By God's own law, not seeing in myself
> A guilty judge condemning the less vile.
> . . . .
> I have forgotten mercy: so might God
> Forget His mercy in my utmost need.
>
> (168)

This speech confuses Henry, and he seeks to shift his talk with Anne to the question of another "sin, of grosser cast" (169). Here Anne asserts the truth of her innocence, and Henry,

who knows she is telling the truth, calls the "base report" of
Anne's adultery "the light mintage of some idle tongue" (169).
Together Anne and Henry recall the early days of their love,
and it does seem, as Henry earlier said, that "all shall be well"
for Anne (135). But the reestablished love between Anne and
Henry does not last; and for the reasons already discussed Henry's public accusation dooms her. Once the conflict within Henry
is settled, the play focuses on the development of Anne's understanding and acceptance of her fate.

That understanding, which develops gradually during the
play, begins with Anne's soliloquy on time in act 3, scene 2.
Throughout her life Anne has sought to master time. To master
time is to make it meaningful. Instead of living from moment
to moment, the one who masters time seeks to impose a pattern
on it so that each moment brings one nearer some final goal.
Mistakenly, Anne has sought to master time in order to achieve,
and to achieve dishonorably, earthly power. Unfortunately, once
one loses earthly power time becomes nothing more than a
series of meaningless moments leading to death. By this scene
(3.2) time for Anne is "one confuséd mass," "one eternal present"; and life itself is "mere existence" (153). Death, under
such circumstances, simply confirms life's meaninglessness; it
becomes "that one door" through which a person leaves the
"labyrinth of cunning thought" (154) that is the life of Henry's
court, the life to which Anne has dedicated herself.

Ironically, to seek to master time as Anne has done results
not in order, but disorder, and makes life not meaningful, but
meaningless. Yet to say that Anne's seeking to impose order
upon her life was a mistake is not to say that once she falls
from power she ought to drift passively with events. Such inac-
tion, as Anne correctly realizes, makes people "mere puppets
of a rigid fate" (154). If attempting to subdue fate is a mistake,
so too is merely becoming fate's puppet. Thus Anne pleads in
this scene for "fate-subduing power" that will carry her through
"One struggle more to master coming time" (154).

At this point, Anne pleads, as she has done before, for the
power to defeat her enemies at their own game. But as she
later sees, the struggle "to master coming time" is not a struggle
to control events at Henry's court. One cannot control fate, if
by control one means bending fate to one's purpose, for fate
is more powerful than man. Fortune's wheel falls as inevitably

as it rises; and if nothing else destroys man's attempt to master fortune, death will.

"To master coming time" one must align oneself with a higher order. In *Anne Boleyn,* then, Boker imagines two contrasting orders, or fates: the temporal order of fortune and the eternal order Anne calls the "grand harmony" (191). The contrast Boker uses here is similar to that found in such "Christian trage- dies" as T. S. Eliot's *Murder in the Cathedral* and Jean Anouilh's *Becket;* and *Anne Boleyn* rests on many of the same paradoxes as do these works. Paradoxically, in seeking to master fortune, one is mastered; and death is fortune's victory over man's at- tempt to master time. Paradoxically, submission to the "grand harmony" is freedom, and death now becomes a means of defeat- ing time. Further, submission is action, not passivity, and re- quires that a hero or heroine possess what Anne describes as "the conscious power / By which the guiltless bear their martyr- dom" (200).

To achieve this "power," Anne must resist the temptations fortune presents. She must resist, first, the temptation of striking at Henry directly by supporting a rebellion. Not only would such a course deny Anne's love for Henry, but it would also return her to the world of intrigue, to the "labyrinth of cunning thought." Second, Anne must resist insanity. On the face of it, insanity may not seem a temptation, but in this play it is, for insanity represents a means by which Anne may escape her suffering.

Anne has good reasons for allowing herself such an escape. She cannot understand why Henry, who loved her, acts dishon- estly toward her. She fears for her reputation after her death, and this fear, as well as her increasing concern for her friends, troubles her. She is powerless to defend herself even though she knows she is innocent of adultery, and Wyatt's attempts to save her prove useless. She is surrounded by spies who tor- ment her, and she feels increasingly guilty for her part in the sufferings of Catherine and Wolsey.

But insanity is the wrong kind of response, for to become insane is to submit to fortune. Insanity is passivity and is, there- fore, the opposite of "the conscious power." This "conscious power," which is not the illusory "inborn power" Anne invoked in the first act, refers both to Anne's awareness that she is inno- cent and to her insights into the nature of fortune and her

earlier life. Anne's "conscious power" is her ability to hold
all she experiences and all she learns, to endure "this watchful
agony of rigid sense" (213) without going insane. It represents
her attempt to retain her freedom of will. As she asks Sir William
Kingston, her jailer, "What but free will is freedom?" (206).

Anne's "conscious power" and her freedom of will make
her a foil to Henry. As the tournament scene (4.1) shows, Henry's apparent freedom to pursue whatever whims he chooses
is illusory. Not only do his actions in this scene trap him in
the events he is trying to control, but his actions are a deliberate
attempt to escape free will, and hence responsibility, by placing
himself in a situation where he can no longer choose between
courses of action. Henry's insight, his consciousness, gives him
no power to alter his life, and he is finally a passive actor in
this play. It is Henry who becomes the "puppet" of fortune.
Anne's power, on the other hand, gives her awareness enough
to resist the snares of fortune and enables her to make the
heroic speeches at her trial and execution.

The originality of these speeches does not lie in Boker's poetic
ability, since he makes few changes in the speeches he found
in Strickland's account. But Boker should be credited with having integrated these speeches into his play so that they form a
natural and inevitable climax. In the last line of the play, for
example, Anne asks that "The Lord have pity on [her] helpless
soul" (234). At her death Anne is a far different character from
the one who claimed at the outset to be "A poor nerveless
woman" at heaven's mercy; and Boker has shown how Anne's
character has developed and how she has achieved her final
dignity. Similarly, when she earlier believed that she could control fortune, Anne asserted that her decline would "blaze" and
that she would "show the world a spectacle more grand" than
when she rose to power (128–29). By the play's end, she has
shown "the world a spectacle more grand," and Boker has
shown how she has achieved that "spectacle."

Anne Boleyn represents Boker's first successful attempt to write
an historical drama, a play in which "art [is] bounded and working within the limits of history."[10] It is also his first successful
examination of his central theme of the individual's conflict with
society. In *Anne Boleyn*, as in *Leonor de Guzman* and *Francesca
da Rimini*, Boker does not make this conflict either simple or
one-sided. Anne is no innocent victim of her society, for she

is herself guilty of having lived by her society's code. What is more important, she is tied to her society, and to its most corrupt member, by love and loyalty. She cannot, like Calaynos, seek to escape physically; nor can her society be defeated except through martydom. Yet, even late in the play, Boker does not make Anne eager for death. While she regards death as a release from her trials, Anne is still attached to this world; and by making that attachment convincing, Boker makes her the first of several characters who, crushed by their societies, are unwilling as well as unable to escape the forces that destroy them.

Anne's martydom, however, is more than an heroic triumph over the world of fortune. While Boker does not suggest that her martydom revolutionizes society, he does suggest that it quietly affects the course of human progress and that it does so because of the artist.

In *Anne Boleyn* Boker uses Wyatt as a means of examining the theme of the artist's duty. Once more, history provided Boker with a detail—Wyatt's presence during these events— that he transforms into art. Historically, Wyatt's role in these events is at best ambiguous. He himself had courted Anne, who was his cousin, and may have been her lover. It is likely that he gave over pursuing her either when Henry objected or when it became obvious that to pursue her would be politically dangerous. At the time of Anne's imprisonment in 1536, Wyatt was himself imprisoned, but managed to win back Henry's friendship, something he managed to do again when he was imprisoned for treason in 1541. While in such a satire as "Mine own John Poins" Wyatt criticizes the hypocrisy and intrigue of court life, he seems to have been skillful at surviving those intrigues.

In Boker's play, however, Wyatt is portrayed as an artist who, like Anne, must learn that the power of human beings to control a corrupt society is limited. Through much of the play Wyatt seeks, first, to warn Anne and her friends of their danger and, second, to instigate a rebellion. But like Anne, Wyatt must learn to accept her martydom. He must learn that he cannot stop the forces of fortune:

> I feel my weakness to support her cause,
> Against the pampered monster of a king—
> This frightful idol of the people's will,

Throned on the superstitious reverence
Of the poor fools that glut his savage maw.
O, what a curse to have an honest heart,
Hemmed in and cramped by the fixed frame of things.
(178–79)

Only as an artist does Wyatt have any power, and that power is over the future, not the present.

As Boker suggested in "Pre-eminence of the Man of Letters," society's future hope depends on man's gradual development of insight and conscience, and the artist's duty is to contribute to that development. Within *Anne Boleyn* itself, Anne's death is affecting the common people by making them question the type of government they have. But if Anne's memory dies, or if it becomes entombed in what Wyatt calls "frigid chronicles" (231), then any hope of progress based on her experience also dies. Thus Wyatt must keep her memory alive not, he says, by directly telling her story, but by hinting at it in his poems:

I'll hide thy name
Under the coverture of even lines,
I'll hint it darkly in familiar songs,
I'll mix each melancholy thought of thee
Through all my numbers.
(232)

For obvious reasons, Boker could not have Wyatt claim that he would treat Anne directly in his poetry. But Wyatt's statements are meant to show that his works, whatever their subject, were inspired by contemporary events and were to have contemporary significance. To extend this idea to Boker's play does not mean that one should seek references to the nineteenth century in *Anne Boleyn*. It does mean that whatever the subject of his plays, Boker sought to portray the unchanging and eternal meaning of an event, and his aim was to awaken his audience to that truth.

As *Anne Boleyn* shows, such an approach did not lead Boker to a simplistic didacticism. The "truth" of *Anne Boleyn* is complex. Her relationship with her society, her own innocence and guilt, and her final actions do not represent simple answers to what is, in fact, a complex matter. They do represent a more successful treatment of the questions and problems Boker raised in *Calaynos* and to which he would return in *Leonor de Guzman.*

The Comedies

Leonor de Guzman followed a period in Boker's career during which he experienced some measure of the fame his early tragedies failed to bring. In 1850, disappointed because *Anne Boleyn* was not staged and because none of his works had excited much attention among the reading public, he began writing comedies. Between *Anne Boleyn* and *Leonor de Guzman*, he completed *The Betrothal* (1850); *The World a Mask* (1851); and *The Widow's Marriage* (1852). Then following *Leonor de Guzman* and in the same year as *Francesca da Rimini*, he completed *The Bankrupt* (1853), a melodrama whose situations and denouement resemble those of the comedies. In his comedies, including *The Bankrupt,* Boker deliberately attempted to please popular taste, and—in a sense—he succeeded. The comedies were more popular than the first two tragedies, and even *The Widow's Marriage,* the only comedy not produced, was kept off the stage solely because no actress could play the lead.

But while he found his comedies were more popular than his tragedies, writing the comedies was anything but a happy experience. As might be expected, writing directly for the stage was frustrating to Boker, and his letters to Bayard Taylor between 1850 and 1853 complain of the changes he must make in his plays and of the kinds of plays he must write. Boker did not think his comedies significant, and, when it came, the very fame he desired confirmed his judgment. Since he recognized that a play like *The World a Mask* was a bad play badly acted, he could neither understand nor take seriously the applause it won for its stage-worthiness and literary quality. His tragedies, which he thought important, were ignored while his comedies were praised, and Boker's disdain for his fame as a playwright sprang from his disgust at the shallowness of popular taste.

Boker's assessment of his comedies' relative insignificance is accurate. He was not a comic writer, and his comedies have little intrinsic merit. In part, Boker never found a type of comedy he could make his own. Like his tragedies, his comedies imitate earlier plays, particularly the romantic comedies of Shakespeare and the social comedies of Sheridan. While his tragedies have some depth, he was unable to match that depth in his comedies. Nor could he make them "sparkle." His wit, as is the case when his tragedies strive for comic relief, is labored; his satire conventional and trivial. Boker's imagination, in other words, could not create comedies that were alive and lively.

Furthermore, as he wrote his comedies, Boker encountered still other problems his imagination could not solve. Their subject matter brought him progressively closer to the contemporary world, and he could not convincingly portray that world. Comedy also forced him to seek a new style, a new language, for his contemporary characters, and he could find no language to take the place of his usual "Shakespearian" rhetoric. As a result, Boker's attempt to write comedies failed, and that failure explains why romantic tragedy, which Boker initially adopted for reasons already discussed, remained the only genre in which he could work.

The Betrothal, his first comedy, is closest to his tragedies in setting and theme. It is a romantic comedy, which means both that it is set in an exotic place and the indeterminate past and that it presents the triumph of love over evil. The Marquis di Tiburzzi, father of the heroine, Costanza, is an impoverished and debt-ridden aristocrat who lives in a ruined castle. To gain money, the Marchioness convinces the Marquis that Costanza wishes to marry Marsio, a deformed and evil merchant who, having money, wants a position in Tuscan society. The Marquis agrees to the marriage, and Costanza, tricked into believing that her father wishes it, also agrees.

After agreeing to the marriage, however, Costanza meets Juanario, who, in addition to being rich, has the further advantages of being young, handsome, and noble. Their meeting takes place in a park, an idyllic setting associated with the harmony of nature and contrasted with the corrupt world of Tuscany. To insure that Costanza cannot marry Juanario, Marsio acquires the Marquis's debts and—adding a note of melodrama to the play— threatens to send the old, sick Marquis to jail if Costanza fails to go through with the wedding.

The play's major action is the successful attempt of Juanario's friends to outwit Marsio. They do this by making Marsio believe he has drunk a poison he intended for Juanario. In fact, Marsio drinks an opiate that makes him believe he is dying. But since Marsio did plot to murder Juanario, he is a criminal and must give up his claim to the Marquis's debts as well as his claim to Costanza in order to escape punishment. Since Juanario and Costanza are then free to marry and since the Marquis is saved from ruin, the play ends happily.

Although Marsio's desire for social prominence might have led Boker to satirize either Marsio himself or the society he wishes to enter, Boker's principal concern in *The Betrothal* is not social satire, though satire is present. Like the world of the tragedies, the world of *The Betrothal* is split between noble and ignoble forces—between the world of Costanza's park and the Marquis's ruined castle—and evil in this play is a Machiavellian force that must be expelled rather than reformed or ridiculed. Marsio's flaw is not his desire to enter society, but his method of fulfilling that desire. As the Marquis says, Marsio fails to understand that a gulf exists between a criminal, however rich, "And the frank brotherhood of honest men, / However poor."[11] For all its apparent decay and corruption, Tuscan society rests on this ideal and not, as Marsio assumes, on the mere possession of wealth.

Like *The Betrothal*, *The World a Mask* imagines a world from which a villain must be expelled, but here that expulsion requires that one of the play's good characters achieve self-awareness. Moreover, in this play, set in England in 1851, when Boker combines with a romantic plot a certain degree of social satire, he directs it not so much at any particular manners as at the characters' inability to distinguish between apparent and real nobility and merit. Rylton, nephew to Sir Hugh Blumer, loves Lucy Willburg. Galldove, another nephew and the villain, circulates rumors about Rylton, thereby hoping to estrange Rylton from Sir Hugh and to win Lucy for himself. To gain admission to society, Galldove is traveling with Teresa Cespo. Teresa, the long-lost sister of Rylton's friend Fernwood, pretends to be a countess, and society's ready acceptance of her apparent nobility is meant to be the object of satire. Boker, however, is unable either to realize the comic possibilities inherent in this mixture of *Twelfth Night* and *The School for Scandal* or to create a well-defined society to satirize.

While not a successful play, *The World a Mask* is Boker's

most complex comedy, and that complexity arises from his handling of the romantic plot. During the writing of the play Boker said that although he "started to make the play a comedy, . . . the serious element" kept "crawling in" (LT, October 15, 1850). The most "serious element" is Galldove's threat to Rylton and Lucy's relationship, and Galldove's ability to pose that threat rests on Teresa's complicity in his plot. We are led at first to believe that Galldove has seduced Teresa and that she remains with him rather than risk becoming a social outcast. But Teresa remains with Galldove because she loves him, and the play traces her gradual understanding of Galldove's true character and hence of her own delusion. In this comedy, then, Boker creates one character who is a mixture of good and evil, perception and blindness, and who, by coming to understand herself, can insure the happiness of others.

Having written a romantic comedy and then a comedy in which the romantic and satiric elements are more or less balanced, Boker turned to a predominately satiric comedy in *The Widow's Marriage* (1852). Here Boker creates a central character, Lady Goldstraw, who strives to appear young. Actually an aging widow, Lady Goldstraw succeeds only in making herself ridiculous, and Boker directs his satire both at her delusion and at the silliness of the fops who play on that delusion in the hope of marrying her for her money.

While satire dominates *The Widow's Marriage*, Boker is still concerned with the triumph of love, since Lady Goldstraw's mistaken belief affects more than her own well-being. Unable to admit she is old, she must maintain the fiction that her daughter, Madge, is too young to fall in love. Consequently, until Lady Goldstraw achieves self-understanding, Madge cannot find her own happiness. Like Teresa, the deluded Lady Goldstraw can find happiness for herself and free others to find their happiness by learning, and accepting, who she is.

In *The Bankrupt* (1853) the romantic elements once more dominate the action, although here those elements are almost overwhelmed by melodrama. Like *The World a Mask, The Bankrupt* is set in Boker's time; unlike the earlier play, it takes place in the United States. *The Bankrupt* treats a rich businessman, Edward Giltwood, who is driven almost to bankruptcy and suicide by his supposed friend James Shelvill. Trying to avenge himself for wrongs suffered long before the play opens, Shelvill seeks not only to ruin Giltwood, but also to destroy Giltwood's marriage by making Amy Giltwood appear unfaithful. Incensed by his wife's apparent faithlessness, Giltwood orders her and "her" children from the house. Nonetheless, Amy is able to save her husband's financial, and her moral, integrity; and Pike, a detective who has pursued Shelvill for three years and who is the source of most of the play's humor, is at last able to arrest Shelvill.

The *Bankrupt* is unquestionably Boker's worst play, and its failure might be attributed to nothing more than the weaknesses inherent in its genre. In effect, this is Edward Bradley's explanation. "Like most surviving plays of this type," he writes, *The Bankrupt* "is deficient in reality of character, artificial in dialogue and extravagant in situation."[12] Yet while this explanation helps to account for the play's failure, the same criticisms could be made of Boker's early tragedies. Although characters in the tragedies are more complex, they are not entirely convincing. Moreover, the "extravagant" elements in *The Bankrupt* had appeared in Boker's other plays, particularly *Calaynos,* and would appear again in *Leonor de Guzman* and *Francesca da Rimini;* and throughout all of his tragedies the language is "artificial." Rather than unique to the genre, then, the weaknesses in *The Bankrupt* may be found in Boker's better plays, and the question becomes why, relative to those plays, this one fails.

For one thing, like *The World a Mask, The Bankrupt* forced Boker to forego the advice he gave Richard Stoddard: "get out of your own age as much as you can" (LS, January 7, 1850). As shown earlier, Boker adopted this position partly because he felt he was following the example of Shakespeare and partly because he felt America lacked literary materials. The comedies show that, in addition to these conscious reasons, Boker's strategy of selecting exotic settings and distant times freed him from what was for him the insurmountable difficulty of creating a specific time and place.

Although his tragedies are set in different countries and at different times, there is little contained in them to suggest a particular locale. Aside from the characters' names and the custom of hating Moors, *Calaynos* could be set as easily in Anne's England, Costanza's Tuscany, or Francesca's Italy as in Spain.

Like its time, the play's setting is indeterminate. But when, as in *The World a Mask* and *The Bankrupt,* the setting was no longer vaguely foreign and the time no longer simply the past, Boker's imagination could not create contemporary characters, have them move in a world recognizably like his own, and use them as the means of expressing "poetical thoughts."

His inability to create a specific time and place is related to the second difficulty he faced in comedy. As his plays' settings and characters became more contemporary, Boker was unable to find a language his characters could speak. That he searched for such a language is indicated, first, by the plays themselves. *The World a Mask,* where Boker first adopted a contemporary setting, is in both prose and blank verse; *The Bankrupt* is entirely in prose. Second, in 1851 Boker wrote Taylor that he was "sick of writing 'in the best style of the old dramatists' " and that he hoped "to strike out" on his own "dramatic path" (LT, January 14, 1851).

In *The World a Mask* the only alternative Boker saw to " 'the best style of the old dramatists' " was to include both blank verse and prose within the same play. Since he was trying to create a "real" society, he could not very well have his characters speak in blank verse. But for Boker a play was a vehicle for expressing eternal truth. Writing to Stoddard in 1852, he discussed the question of whether *"poetical* thoughts may . . . be expressed in prose." For Boker, the answer was no: "Poetry, painting, sculpture, and music are different forms for expressing the same family of ideas" and, just as the latter three cannot be expressed in prose, so too "poetical thought" can be expressed in no other medium (LS, May 21, 1852).

Thus *The World a Mask* adopts blank verse when Boker seeks to express "poetical thought." Galldove, for example, speaks prose through much of the play; but Galldove is meant to be a study of evil and, at those times when he is most villainous, he speaks in blank verse. Similarly, when Fernwood and Teresa discuss their childhood, which Teresa remembers as a paradise she had to leave as she grew older, they speak in blank verse. And at the end, when harmony is established and the trivial moral drawn, blank verse is again Boker's medium.

Having combined blank verse and prose in *The World a Mask,* he returned to blank verse for *The Widow's Marriage.* But this play takes place in 1730 and is not an attempt to portray the mid-nineteenth century. In *The Bankrupt,* however, Boker once more wrote a play that required something other than blank verse, and this time he settled exclusively on prose. Still, when Shelvill opens the play by announcing his villainy, he speaks not ordinary prose, but a cadenced, "poetic" prose that is typical of the play's major characters:

Ten years ago, city of sin and misery, you drove me from you for a crime of which I was guiltless; now I return to you, after a career that would make your early charge seem lenient. Ten years ago, I left you poor, persecuted, yet innocent; now I return to you rich, powerful, yet guilty. I will make you sob in your houses, and lament in your streets! I will cram you with new grief, until it equal my old sorrow! Woe! to you who trampled upon my heart![13]

While this speech may immediately strike a reader as "melo-dramatic," it is striving for the effect blank verse had made in Boker's earlier tragedies. But judging by his comments to Stod-dard, Boker must have found making prose poetic even less satisfactory than alternating prose and poetry. "What is more disgusting," he asked, "than 'poetical prose'? It produces the same effect upon me as a wax figure in the place of a statue. You feel in reading it that the form is wrong." As though he were looking ahead to Shelvill's speech, Boker adds that a writer of such prose "always . . . introduces some kind of cadence, by which he in a measure imitates the natural rhythm of poetry" (LS, May 21, 1852).

The theatrical conventions of Boker's time did not provide him with a vehicle for expressing "poetical thought," and he did not try to create one. For Boker, to leave "the best style of the old dramatists" meant either to alternate that style with prose or to write "poetical prose" and while neither alternative was satisfactory, the second was especially distasteful. "With me," he said of "poetical prose," "the cheat never answers; I feel the whole thing to be a sham, and despise it as such" (LS, May 21, 1852)—so much so, in fact, that Boker did not acknowl-edge *The Bankrupt* when it opened in 1855 and did not include either it or *The World a Mask* among the works published in 1856. They were not, in his eyes, poetical works; and for the reasons outlined here, comedy had proven an impossible form.

Leonor de Guzman

Frustrated by writing comedies, Boker returned to romantic tragedy in 1852. Drawing upon Prosper Mérimée's *History of Pedro the Cruel* (1849) and Anita George's *Annals of the Queens of Spain* (1850), he dramatized the story of Leonor de Guzman. Leonor, the mistress of the Spanish king Alfonso XII, lived with Alfonso for many years in Medina Sidonia and bore him three sons. Shortly after the play begins, Leonor learns that the king has died of the plague. With Alfonso dead, she and her sons, all of whom are adults, are in danger from their political enemies, who could not strike at Leonor so long as Alfonso lived. The play focuses on Leonor's attempt to protect her sons by marrying her eldest, Enrique, to her ward Juana. Since Juana belongs to a powerful family, the marriage will legitimate Leonor's sons and provide them with powerful allies.

Leonor's plan is opposed by Albuquerque, the prime minister, who hopes to marry Juana to Alfonso's legitimate son Pedro. To overcome that opposition, Leonor must return to the court at Seville. There she is confronted not only by Albuquerque, but also by Maria, Alfonso's wife, who hates Leonor and wishes her dead. In spite of Albuquerque and Maria, Leonor arranges a secret marriage between Enrique and Juana. She has, however, only a brief time to enjoy her triumph before Maria murders her.

The story of Leonor de Guzman provided Boker with yet another vehicle for treating his major theme. Leonor's behavior defies social convention, and she must struggle with a corrupt world. As his earlier plays show, the theme of the individual and society raised for Boker primarily five questions: To what extent can the individual overcome society and establish a new world? To what kind of new world can an individual flee? From what kind of world is he or she fleeing? What is gained and lost both by the person and by society at large when an individual rebels against convention? Is the reformation of society a possibility?

While all his earlier plays examined one or another of these questions, Boker lacked the skill to explore all of them fully in any single work. At times, of course, he failed to explore any one of them consistently throughout a given play. By the time he wrote *Leonor de Guzman,* though, he had the skill necessary to sustain a full examination of his theme. As a result, *Leonor de Guzman* raises all the issues that had intrigued him before.

Leonor de Guzman opens in Medina Sidonia, where Leonor has established a court opposed to the legitimate court at Seville. Early in the play Leonor describes how she turned what was essentially chaos into a pastoral enclave based upon honor:

> I found this land an arméd wilderness,
> A chain of citadels, and all between
> Was desolation trampled into dust.
>
> . . . .
>
> So, in the midst, I built a house of peace,
> An unwalled palace, full of open doors;
> And round about I spread a garden-plot,
> Hedged it with flowers, and from its sculptured urns
> I sent the streams back to their native heaven,
> Returned in music. No defence was mine,
> Save the imploring weakness of the flowers.[14]

Medina Sidonia recalls both Calaynos's estate and Costanza's park. In addition, through the imagery of nature and music, it recalls Anne Boleyn's description of her childhood and Teresa's of hers in *The World a Mask.* Like all of these, Medina Sidonia is an ideal world removed from the "real" world, and early in *Leonor de Guzman* Boker raises the issue of the kind of ideal world Leonor has established.

Appropriately, the worlds Anne and Teresa remember are the unambiguously ideal places each inhabited before encountering life's complexity: they are childhood paradises each has had to give up and to which each looks back with longing. Similarly, Costanza's park is an earthly paradise—Juanario's description of Costanza's tending the park recalls the prelapsarian Eve in *Paradise Lost*—but it is a paradise in which Costanza can escape the corruption of Tuscany and which, by the play's end, has triumphed over that corruption. In *Calaynos,* however, Boker made Calaynos's estate an ambiguous place. Theoretically established because of Calaynos's love of truth and his fellowman, the estate removes Calaynos from mankind. His love is a cold, intellectual love that leaves a specific human being, such as Lady Alda, isolated and bored.

Like Calaynos's estate, then, Medina Sidonia is not a purely ideal place. Leonor may say that flowers were her only weapons in establishing this world, but the honor on which Medina Sidonia rests is, for two reasons, ambiguous.

First, Leonor's innocent world depends on the political reality of Alfonso's presence. Like Anne's, Leonor's power and safety depend on a king's remaining loyal to her. The courtiers do not remain at Medina Sidonia because of an unwavering loyalty to Leonor, let alone to peace and harmony, but because as long as Alfonso lives, Leonor's court is the center of power. As soon as Alfonso dies, Leonor recognizes that he was "the noble tree from which / Castilian honor drew its only sap" (253). While alive, he had nourished those who, once he is gone, will transfer their loyalties elsewhere. After he dies and the courtiers see that Leonor will not try to seize the crown, they flee to Seville, which they assume will be the new center of power, and the ideal world of this play is powerless to survive the first act.

Second, Medina Sidonia rests on the adulterous relationship between Alfonso and Leonor. Leonor's being an adulteress is, like Calaynos's race, an arbitrary convention that serves as the basis of society's judgment of the individual. But the adultery is far richer in thematic implications than was Calaynos's race. In part, the adultery looks forward to the adultery in *Francesca da Rimini* and represents an individual's defiance of social conventions and, through that defiance, the individual's attempt to find a happiness the social order denies. While the social order, particularly the church, may condemn Leonor's adultery, she defends it on the grounds that a higher law than that of the church has sanctioned the relationship. Asked by her confessor late in the play if she repents of "the sinful tie," Leonor asserts that that "tie— / The pure connection of two faithful hearts," was "something holier, something nearer heaven, / Than aught the church has gathered from above" (326). Told that such an attitude insures her damnation—and Leonor is afraid of hell—she still defends her adultery:

> There is no creed for this, no law, I own,
> Save that which nature whispers in our ears;
> And, in her whisper, pardon if I thought
> I heard the still small voice.
>
> (326)

Heaven may judge her as it will; Leonor has acted "According to the light within her soul" (326).

In *Leonor de Guzman*, however, the adultery is no more an unambiguous throwing off of the world's corrupt restrictions than is Hester and Dimmesdale's adultery in *The Scarlet Letter;* Leonor herself is fully aware of the affair's ambiguity. Her attempt to achieve happiness by defying the social order is limited by the power of the social order itself. In *Calaynos* Boker attempted to show the power of the social order only by having Don Luis, for reasons of his own, enter Calaynos's ideal world and destroy it. In *Anne Boleyn* Boker again briefly touched on this aspect of his theme by showing that Henry's court is too powerful for Anne to defeat. In *Leonor de Guzman* the inability of Alfonso and Leonor to escape completely the force of the world around them is clearly defined. For Leonor, marriage to Alfonso, not adultery, would have been the more ideal relationship; and in the play, as in history, Leonor is offered the opportunity of having Alfonso divorce Maria. But she recognizes that a divorce is not politically possible since the King of Portugal, Maria's father, would no longer remain Castile's ally. Medina Sidonia is, therefore, not the best of all possible worlds; in the best world Alfonso and Leonor would have married. Adultery is the price Leonor has had to pay in order to achieve what measure of happiness she could.

Moreover, the adultery is ambiguous because, as Leonor is also aware, her attempt to fulfill her sense of self has implications for, and involves, the well-being of others. In his earlier plays Boker had shown that Calaynos's attempt to realize his ideals places Lady Alda in a position that finally destroys her and that Anne's relationship with Henry required that Catherine suffer.

Similarly, the adultery of Alfonso and Leonor entails suffering for Maria.

It would have been easy enough to have portrayed Maria as a monster who deserves no better treatment than Leonor and Alfonso inflict on her; but Boker does not do this. While her hatred of Leonor has become an obsession, Maria has reasons for that hatred, and her assertions that she loved Alfonso, whether or not he loved her, and her description of her lonely years at Seville make her murder of Leonor more pathetic than villainous. Leonor herself respects Maria's position in society, for early in the play she rebukes those who insult Maria. And while Leonor will not repent of the adultery itself, she twice repents of the pain it caused Maria.

Finally, in Boker's plays characters of noble rank have obligations to the world at large, a kind of *noblesse oblige,* and Leonor is aware of her obligations. Again, Boker had touched on this aspect of his theme earlier. Calaynos feels an obligation to aid the poor of his region, and Anne feels a duty to protect the order of the state. By refusing to sanction a rebellion against Henry, Anne loses any hope of escaping execution. But she refuses to support Wyatt's rebellion not only because a rebellion would violate her love for Henry, but also because it would threaten the order of the state. For both Anne and Leonor, that order, whatever its limitations, is better than anarchy.

Even before Alfonso's death, Leonor will do nothing that threatens the welfare of Seville. Hence she refuses to entertain the idea of a divorce, and she will not approve any plan to make her queen. At one time in her life Leonor says that she might have acted otherwise. But having spent "many a painful hour of solemn thought" and having struggled "with a treacherous heart, / Whose passions threatened to be paramount," Leonor now has ambitions for "No title in the spacious gift of man, / Above the welfare of her native land" (248). Following Alfonso's death, she urges her sons to arm themselves for their own protection—to do otherwise would be foolish—but there are to be "No swords" for Leonor herself (252). Instead, faithful to the ideals represented by Medina Sidonia, she will journey to Seville where she hopes that what she later calls "the voice / Of nature" will plead for her sons (275).

At the end of the first act of *Calaynos* Calaynos must journey to Seville; at the end of the first act of *Leonor de Guzman* Leonor makes the same journey. In both plays the journey marks the start of the rising action, but in *Calaynos* the relationship between the journey and the elements of the theme is tenuous at best. A measure of Boker's achievement in *Leonor de Guzman* is his ability to draw the strands of his theme together in order to motivate Leonor's actions. In part, Leonor must accompany Alfonso's body simply because of her love for him. Having been loyal to him "through life," she will "follow through the shades of death" (254). In part, Leonor must go to Seville because, without Alfonso, there is no realistic basis for Medina Sidonia's continued existence. Seeing that Leonor will not support a struggle with Seville, the courtiers desert, and Leonor recognizes that Medina Sidonia is not strong enough to survive against Seville. And finally, only in Seville can Leonor fulfill her ambition of protecting her sons. The journey to Seville is in part, then, a confirmation of her love for Alfonso; in part, a recognition of Medina Sidonia's limitations and of the necessity of returning to the "real" world; and in part, an attempt to bring the ideals of Medina Sidonia into that world.

Having examined Medina Sidonia in the first act, Boker turns his attention in the second to the nature of Seville. In *Calaynos* and *Anne Boleyn* the two tragic figures confronted worlds that were entirely corrupt. The Seville in *Leonor de Guzman* is not. Although he is weak and easily duped by Albuquerque, Don Pedro is an honorable character as well as the rightful heir to the throne. He is, in other words, not yet Pedro the Cruel. He demands that his father's memory be honored. When told by his mother that he should hate Alfonso since Alfonso never loved him, Don Pedro replies that his father's failure to love him gives him more reason to mourn his father's death. Had Alfonso lived, "Time and good actions might have won his love" (269). In addition, provided with an opportunity to destroy Leonor and her sons, Don Pedro refuses on the grounds that the sons are his half brothers and that Leonor's fate should depend on her future actions, not on her past adultery with Alfonso.

Furthermore, Albuquerque, who actually holds the power in Castile, is neither, like Norfolk, simply lusting for "power, power, power" nor, like Don Luis and Henry, trying to placate

a guilty conscience. Instead, like Leonor, Albuquerque seeks
to impose some order on a corrupt world:

> Look at the state in which I found Castile!—
> A kingdom veined and arteried with plots,
> Flowing and ebbing, crossing and recrossing,
> Through every corner of her wide domain.
>
> (281)

But whereas Leonor sought to establish an orderly world
based on honor, Albuquerque, as he tells Maria, uses whatever
devices are necessary to save Castile from anarchy:

> I tell you now—
> Even while I hold these elements in check—
> That if King Pedro die, or I but slack
> My rigid grasp, Castile shall see a storm
> To which mere chaos would be harmony.
>
> (281)

It is true that Albuquerque holds "these elements in check"
to achieve power for himself; and since Leonor threatens that
power, he seeks to destroy her. But the order Albuquerque
has established is not without value. He recognizes that Castile
is on the verge of civil war. He knows that Don Pedro's political
astuteness is limited; that Maria has no interest other than to
see Leonor dead—no matter the cost to the state; and that,
thanks in part to the adultery, several claimants to the throne
are waiting to strike. As Albuquerque realizes, were Don Pedro
to die or were Albuquerque himself to "slack / [His] rigid
grasp," the resulting disorder would be "a storm, / To which
mere chaos would be harmony."

Once Leonor arrives in Seville, the action centers on her
arrangement of the marriage between Enrique and Juana. Although achievement of the marriage will cost Leonor her life,
she, like Anne, triumphs over the world around her. In *Anne
Boleyn* Anne's triumph is figurative rather than literal. She
achieves a dignity by the time the play ends that makes her
more heroic and noble than her enemies. But history provided
Boker with no means for Anne to triumph literally. She is destroyed by her enemies, but they remain little affected by her.

In *Leonor de Guzman,* on the other hand, history did provide a means whereby Boker could show that Leonor triumphs both figuratively and literally. Like Anne, Leonor achieves heroic dignity at her death. Despite her rebellion against convention, she regrets the pain she has caused Maria. But while she repents for some of her earlier life, she asserts, even as she dies, the sanctity of her love for Alfonso.

Literally, Leonor triumphs by effecting the marriage between Enrique and Juana. Yet nothing in *Leonor de Guzman* is unambiguous. To triumph over Albuquerque through this marriage, Leonor must outwit him by being more adept than he at intrigue. Consequently, when she arrives in Seville, she tells him that she understands his "wily policy and cunning turns." If he meets her with "candor," she will meet him "with like truth." But if he practices the art of deception on her, "art for art, / And scheme for scheme, shall meet [him] everywhere" (278–79). Unlike Anne, who had to rise above "the labyrinth of cunning thought" at Henry's court, Leonor must equal Albuquerque, whom she describes as "a labyrinth so full of guile" (295).

Leonor de Guzman remains a tragedy in spite of Leonor's outwitting of Albuquerque; and for Boker that tragedy lies in the complex and paradoxical nature of Leonor's situation. Whatever choices she makes are both right and wrong, and her ability to fulfill her individual desires is limited. Her love for Alfonso was right; yet under the conventions the play assumes it was also wrong. Her attempt to establish Medina Sidonia was right; yet Medina Sidonia itself is subject to the limitations inherent in human beings and could only be established through adultery. Leonor's attempt to effect the marriage is right; yet that attempt costs her her life and requires that she engage in the deceit of Seville.

At the end of the first act Boker had drawn the strands of his theme together to motivate Leonor's return to Seville. As the play ends, he again touches on those strands, for like everything else about her, Leonor's death is complex. Historically, Maria hired an assassin to murder Leonor. In the play, she commits the murder herself. Hoping that Leonor is unrepentant and will, therefore, be damned, Maria asks if she repents. Leonor replies, as she earlier did to her confessor, that she repents of the "wrongs" she did Maria and, acknowledging her responsibility to society, of "the mischief [her] example" did to the social order; but she remains faithful to her love for Alfonso (342). Afraid of death, and especially of the act of dying, Leonor looks toward the future represented by Enrique and Juana and prophesies the deaths of Maria and Albuquerque. Finally, she looks toward heaven and, using images that recall her earlier description of Medina Sidonia, imagines she sees a "little river" that "steals away." On that river, she says, she will "float to heaven" (345). At the play's end, then, Boker suggests that although Leonor has triumphed, the ambiguities she confronted in life can be reconciled only in death, and the recalling of Medina Sidonia serves to show that the world Leonor desired is possible, if at all, only in heaven.

   Conclusion: The significance of *Leonor de Guzman.* Later history proved Leonor's prophecies concerning Enrique, Maria, and Albuquerque to be correct. Pedro eventually became Pedro the Cruel, and Enrique led a successful rebellion against him. Initially, Boker planned to continue the Guzman's story, and he began a play titled *Don Pedro of Castile.* But he never completed the project and turned instead to *Francesca da Rimini.* That play is better known than *Leonor de Guzman.* Yet in some ways *Leonor de Guzman* is a more successful work. Dramatically stronger than any of his earlier plays, *Leonor de Guzman* is as thematically rich and complex as *Francesca da Rimini.* But as shall be seen, *Francesca da Rimini* cannot sustain its thematic complexity. *Leonor de Guzman* does.

   Of the plays written between 1848 and 1852 *Leonor de Guzman* offers Boker's most perceptive examination of the conflict between the individual and society and is best viewed as a culmination of both the early comedies and the early tragedies. From the beginning Boker tried to show that the individual's conflict with his or her world was more than a melodramatic struggle between innocence and evil. While he had shown that Calaynos was a victim of his society's arbitrary conventions and of that society's inherent corruption, he had tried as well to suggest that Calaynos's response to life was itself flawed and inadequate. In *Anne Boleyn* Boker sought to portray Anne not so much as a victim of society's conventions—nothing in Anne corresponds to Calaynos's being a Moor—but as the victim of a corrupt social order. Yet in that play Boker complicated the issue by showing that Anne is herself inextricably tied to that order and is thus not only unable, but also unwilling, to destroy the order that crushes her.

The character of Leonor combines elements of both Calaynos and Anne Boleyn. Like Calaynos, she wishes to establish a pastoral world; unlike him, she is able to recognize the costs involved in such an attempt. She perceives that an ideal world must have a political foundation, and that entirely escaping the social order is impossible. Like Anne, she is aware of the need for social order and realizes that her ambitions are limited by her responsibility to the larger good. Through much of the play Leonor is offered the option of supporting a direct assault on the world of Seville. She recognizes, however, that that option is an illusion. Boker's vision of the individual's relationship with society is conservative. He sees the individual's desires limited by the ambiguities within the individual. Could Leonor have convinced herself that a marriage with Alfonso would have been worth any cost; could she have convinced herself that her only duty was to realize her own desires, she would have faced an external conflict between her own wishes and those of the world. As the play stands, Leonor's conflict is as much internal as external. Her desire for an honorable world conflicts with her desire for a relationship with Alfonso. Her desire for that relationship conflicts with her sense of responsibility both to Maria and to the world at large. Her desire for the marriage between Enrique and Juana conflicts with her desire to avoid a life of intrigue in Seville. By the play's end Leonor has had to confront the impossibility of living in an ideal world. She has discovered that the human condition requires that she struggle to bring about as much goodness and honor as she can, not in Medina Sidonia, but in Seville.

By making his heroines fully aware of their responsibilities to the world outside themselves, Boker also clearly defined the difference, as he saw it, between noble and ignoble characters. In some ways, his villains are more fascinating than his heroines. This is not unique to Boker; many readers of *Paradise Lost* find Satan more interesting than God. What is most fascinating about Boker's villains, however, is the completeness with which he makes them foils to his noble characters. The noble characters strive to be free. Although both Anne and Leonor spend much of their careers within the plays in prison, each struggles against insanity because she wishes to retain as much freedom as possible. Rather than attempting to escape from life's complexities, the heroines wish to remain aware of them. The villains, on the other hand, seek to escape freedom and attempt to simplify life. Don Luis tries to convince himself that fate compels him to behave as he does. Henry traps himself in events so that his conscience cannot trouble him. Albuquerque, who sees something of the nature of the world and is instrumental in providing Castile with order, is nonetheless trapped by his simplistic notion that mankind is entirely corrupt.

In addition, the villains know no obligation to anything other than their own desires. Don Luis, Henry, and Albuquerque are the dark side of the individual's struggle to fulfill his own ambitions. Don Luis wishes to commit adultery; Henry wishes to pursue a new passion and does so without regard for the cost to England's well-being; Albuquerque wants Don Pedro kept dependent on him for advice so that he, Albuquerque, can continue to rule. Leonor overcame the temptation of allowing her passions to determine her behavior. The villains in Boker's plays make no attempt to rise above their individual desires.

Finally, *Leonor de Guzman* is Boker's fullest examination of the theme of reforming society. In both *Calaynos* and *Anne Boleyn* his treatment of this theme was slight. In *Francesca da Rimini* he again raises the issue, but does not develop it. Since social reform is part of the comic vision, each of Boker's comedies ends with the expulsion, or the reformation, of evil and the establishment of a new order. But Boker was not content with comedy's quick reorganization of the world. In comedy the new social order seems always to lurk just beneath the surface and to be waiting only for the characters to discover themselves and the truth of their world before breaking forth. As a result, some readers regard comedy as less complex, and hence less mature, than tragedy. Certainly Boker held such a view, since he regarded tragedy as the loftiest and most important literary genre.

Great comedies, however, are not simple works. In Shakespeare's comedies, for example, ambiguities and tensions remain after the works end. While the good people are celebrating their marriages and their new-found worlds, the audience still recalls Malvolio or Shylock with the feeling that these figures have been treated rather harshly. While the lovers in *The Merchant of Venice* go off to bed, Antonio is left behind, excluded from the comic world. The order achieved at the end of great comedies is a delicate balance, for great comedies do not give the sense that everything is, or can be, happy.

Boker's comedies are not great plays in part because Boker could not bring enough complexity to his subject matter, and thus the happiness he portrays at the end of his comedies is unbalanced. The best he could do with comedy's vision of a new world brought about through love and self-discovery was to make it part of *Leonor de Guzman,* where he achieves a reconciliation between the ideal and corrupt worlds through the marriage of Enrique and Juana.

Unlike some other American writers, Boker did not regard the mass of people as the source of reform. His "citizens," as he usually calls them, have no more than a vague awareness of what is happening in the world. They are influenced by events without themselves influencing events. For Boker, the members of the nobility, a class that includes the artist, influence history and are, if they choose to be, the instruments of reform. Yet even their influence is slight. Like others of his attitudes, Boker's attitude toward reform was conservative. Reform occurs slowly, and a given individual makes only a slight contribution to it. As he has Albuquerque say, Boker believed that

> perfect government
> Is not the offspring of a single day;
> But, like the greater creatures of the earth,
> Is rounded slowly in the womb of time,
> And brought to light with more extended pains
> Than the less bulky matters of the world.
> (322)

But by successfully outwitting Albuquerque and achieving the marriage, Leonor accomplishes more than a personal triumph over her enemy, for the marriage marks the beginning of a reformed world. Like the love between Leonor and Alfonso, that between Enrique and Juana is true and noble, but their marriage does not involve breaking the moral code or injuring a third party. The marriage, in other words, incorporates the "still small voice" within the context of the social order. Equally important, the marriage is a political union, like the marriage of Alfonso and Maria, and joins the illegitimate son of Alfonso to the established, "legitimate" society. The new order represented by Enrique and Juana is neither an escape into the order represented by Medina Sidonia nor a capitulation to the purely political order represented by Seville. It is instead a reconciliation of Medina Sidonia and Seville and a triumph of love over evil.

The historical material Boker adopted in *Leonor de Guzman* was fortuitous, for it allowed him to make a thorough examination of the themes that had concerned him from the start of his career. It also allowed him, for the only time in his career, to combine the comedic idea of a reformed world and the tragic idea of the individual's destruction at the hands of a corrupt society. The material also enabled Boker to construct a solid stage play that sustains its portrayal of character and theme throughout the five acts. *Leonor de Guzman* represents Boker's most skillful handling of his genre; and at times the play is moving, although as with all of Boker's works a reader's involvement with the play is more intellectual than emotional.

The play contains as well the seeds of *Francesca da Rimini.* All that remained for Boker to do in order to complicate further his treatment of the individual and society was to make his villains even more sympathetic and complex than Albuquerque and Maria, and he attempts this in *Francesca da Rimini.* As that play demonstrates, his skill and intelligence were limited. He never surpassed the accomplishment of *Leonor de Guzman,* and this play deserves to be remembered as his best.

Chapter Three

Francesca da Rimini

Boker wrote *Francesca da Rimini,* his best-known play, during the first three weeks of March, 1853, and was convinced when he finished it that it surpassed anything he had done. "Of course, you know the story," he wrote Stoddard, "every one does; but you . . . do not know it as I have treated it" (LS, March 3, 1853). He had sought to treat the story in a new way, and he felt that, compared with his earlier tragedies, *Francesca da Rimini* was "more dramatic" and "fiercer in its displays of intense passion." Hence, he concluded, "if it be not a great triumph, it will certainly be a great failure" (LS, March 22, 1853).

The most original element in Boker's treatment of the Francesca story is the character of Lanciotto, the husband of Francesca and brother of Paolo; and *Francesca da Rimini* is unique among Boker's works because it treats two tragedies: that of the lovers and that of Lanciotto, the wronged husband and betrayed brother. Because of its treatment of Francesca and Paolo, the play deserves its preeminent place among Boker's works. It is, as he thought, "more dramatic" than his earlier tragedies. In addition, Boker skillfully and consistently creates the characters of Paolo and Francesca, and their tragedy is a final and logical step in his exploration of his central theme. In its handling of the lovers the play may be called a "triumph."

Unfortunately, Boker fails to bring the same skill and consistency to his portrayal of Lanciotto, and this failure is especially unfortunate since Lanciotto dominates the play. Into Lanciotto, however, Boker pours too many, often contradictory, elements, and the confusion in Lanciotto's character makes the play thematically confused as well. In its handling of Lanciotto, then, it is more "a great failure" than "a great triumph."

The Tragedy of Francesca and Paolo

Boker did not exaggerate when he said that everyone knew the story of Francesca and Paolo. Few stories have been as popular as this one, although the historical record itself is not as dramatic as the literary treatments of it. Historically, Francesca, a native of Ravenna, married Lanciotto, a native of Rimini, in 1275. While politically motivated, the marriage was not designed, as in Boker's play, to cement a peace between the two city-states, but rather to pay off a political debt which Guido, Francesca's father, owed Lanciotto. Because he was lame and unattractive, Lanciotto sent his brother Paolo to meet Francesca. Believing Paolo to be Lanciotto, Francesca fell in love with him. Already married, Paolo returned the love, and the two continued their affair until 1285, when Lanciotto learned of it and killed the two lovers.

Although many literary artists treated this historical material, only two influenced Boker. The first, of course, was Dante, whose account of the story immortalized the lovers. In the fifth canto of the *Inferno* Francesca tells Dante how she and Paolo were suddenly overcome with passion while reading about Lancelot and Guinevere and how they were discovered and murdered by Francesca's husband. Throughout his treatment of the story Dante emphasizes the unfortunate fate of the lovers. Hearing how Francesca's husband killed them before they had time to repent, Dante weeps; and told of how their affair began, he faints. Thus, while a writer like Boker saw Francesca and Paolo in conflict with their society—rather in the tradition of Romeo and Juliet—Dante portrays them as pitiable victims of a momentary passion that destroyed them. Francesca calls the author of the book that excited them a panderer, and of her husband, who is not named, she says only that a terrible punishment awaits him. The sole comfort the lovers have is being with one another in hell.

The second influence on Boker was Boccaccio's "Commentary on the *Divine Comedy.*" According to Boccaccio, Gianciotto (Lanciotto in Boker's play) was an intelligent man whose physical deformity belied a sensitive and noble nature, and the marriage between him and Francesca was meant to secure the peace be-

tween Rimini and Ravenna. Paolo, as handsome as his brother
is unattractive, goes to Ravenna in Lanciotto's place and marries
Francesca by proxy. After the wedding night Francesca discovers
who is in fact her husband, but by then it is too late. She and
Paolo are in love and continue their affair. Informed of the
affair by a servant, Gianciotto discovers the lovers together,
kills Francesca accidentally when she stands between him and
Paolo, and then kills Paolo.

In addition to the hint about Lanciotto's character, Boker
adopted a number of elements from Boccaccio to help shape
the plot. Malatesta, Lord of Rimini, and Guido da Polenta, Lord
of Ravenna, have concluded a peace between their two city-
states. Since neither leader trusts the other, they try to insure
the peace by arranging a marriage between their children, Francesca and Lanciotto. While dropping the proxy marriage, Boker's play retains Paolo's being sent to meet Francesca, who
believes she is meeting Lanciotto. The two fall in love, but
resist their passion until the fateful reading scene. Pepe, the
court jester and Boker's most vicious villain, sees the lovers
together and informs Lanciotto. When Lanciotto finds Francesca
and Paolo, he kills Francesca not accidentally, as in Boccaccio,
but deliberately. Paolo, paralyzed by guilt and indecision, refuses to fight Lanciotto, and Lanciotto hopes the death of Francesca will incite Paolo. When Paolo still refuses to fight,
Lanciotto murders him and then dies.

From Dante, Boker retained the pity expressed toward the
lovers—although, typical of romantic treatments of the story,
he changed the terms of that pity. For him, the Francesca story
became a vehicle for presenting the theme of individuals whose
desires are thwarted by the world around them. As Boker treats
it, however, the story is more than that of two innocent and
noble people crushed by a corrupt and indifferent society. While
their society creates the situation that destroys them, Francesca
and Paolo find themselves struggling not so much against their
society as against their own consciences.

At the start of the play Francesca is unaware of the deceit
around her and looks to her father to guide her through the
world. She is troubled by her father's having arranged her marriage, but accepts the marriage as a duty she is willing to

do to please him. "I knew," she says, "that it must be my destiny, / Someday to give my hand without my heart,"[1] and she
is ready "To force affection upon any man / Called Lanciotto"
(388). But her father, unwilling to rely on Francesca's honor
and sense of duty, deceives her by allowing her to believe that
Paolo is Lanciotto. When Francesca discovers the truth, she discovers also her father's "ill usage, gross abuse, / Treason to
duty, meanness, craft—dishonor" (388).

Once she discovers her father's deceit, Francesca finds she
must increasingly rely on her wits in order to survive. After
upbraiding her father for the act, Francesca returns and asks
his forgiveness. She does so out of pity for him, but it is clear
as soon as he leaves that Francesca knows she can no longer
rely on him nor, as the following soliloquy shows, remain where
he is:

> Let me begone [*sic*]:
> I could not look him in the face again
> With the old faith. . . .
>
> . . . .
>
> and I could not trust—
> Strive as I might—my happiness to him,
> As once I did. I could not lay my hand
> Upon his shoulder, and look up to him,
> Saying, Dear father, pilot me along
> Past this dread rock, through yonder narrow strait.
>   (393–94)

Since she has no mother and since her father has betrayed
her, Francesca must look elsewhere for aid. At first, seeking
to discover what Lanciotto is like, she turns to Paolo, who describes his brother's character and accomplishments in glowing
terms while omitting any mention of his appearance. When she
sees Lanciotto, Francesca believes that Paolo, like the rest, has
been dishonest. Even as she meets Lanciotto, Francesca is still
the victim of deceit. Lanciotto, who pities Francesca when he
discovers she has been duped, is willing to let her out of the
bargain and still honor the peace. In a series of asides, however,
Francesca's father, who is using the marriage as a delaying tactic
while he rebuilds his army, tells her not to trust Lanciotto, but

to pledge once more her willingness to marry him. This Francesca does, and her statement to Lanciotto that she freely wishes to marry him leads Lanciotto to believe she in fact loves him; it is her first act of deception:

> Thus I begin the practice of deceit,
> Taught by deceivers, at a fearful cost.
> The bankrupt gambler has become the cheat,
> And lives by arts that erewhile ruined me.
>
> (421)

But at heart Francesca is honest. In a world that requires hypocrisy she cannot be hypocritical. Earlier she had realized she could not live with her father because she could not pretend to be his dutiful and trusting daughter after discovering his dishonesty. Now, while she has said she will marry Lanciotto, she cannot bring herself to say she loves him; after she and Paolo consummate their love, she remarks that to "endure" Lanciotto's "loathsome touch" is unthinkable (466). Isolated from everyone, she must choose between loving Paolo openly or continuing to keep her feelings hidden. Her response to finding that her emotions conflict with her social role is to risk all for love:

> The women of our clime
> Do never give away but half a heart:
> I have not part to give, part to withhold,
> In selfish safety.
>
> (451)

Having given all her love to Paolo, Francesca knows that to be apart from him is impossible. She feels she has risked more in this affair than has Paolo, since he can leave Rimini and spare himself "a little bashful pain" (466). For her, there can be no turning back:

> Paolo, dost thou know what 't is for me,
> A woman—nay, a dame of highest rank—
> To lose my purity? to walk a path
> Whose slightest slip may fill my ear with sounds
> That hiss me out to infamy and death?
>
> (466)

If Paolo is determined to leave Rimini, so too will she. Had she to choose between their love and her former innocence, she tells him, she "would dare again / The deed which we have done" (467).

No such choice is given. The scene is interrupted by Lanciotto who, having learned of the affair, now seeks vengeance. At the play's end Francesca is a heroine worthy of being compared with Anne or Leonor. But, unlike Anne, who had to align herself with the "grand harmony," and unlike Leonor, who accepted her death while maintaining that her affair transcended conventional definitions of morality, Francesca struggles at the end to save her lover. She is willing to murder Lanciotto—she asks Paolo to give her his sword—and, failing that, she tries to assume all the guilt for the affair. Ultimately, Lanciotto kills her in an attempt to rouse Paolo from his lethargy.

Paolo's lethargy in the final scene is the result of guilt and indecision, two things Boker has been developing from the start of the play. At the outset Paolo is a courtier who, like Romeo, is fond simply of being in love. Immediately, however, another side of Paolo is shown, when Pepe announces that Lanciotto is to marry Francesca. Pepe and the courtiers laugh at the proposed marriage. Reacting violently to their laughter, Paolo threatens to kill anyone "Who dares insult [his] brother with a laugh" (352).

Paolo is deeply loyal to his brother and sensitive to Lanciotto's feelings, particularly his feelings about his lameness. Thus, when Paolo finds himself in love with Francesca, his loyalty and sensitivity to Lanciotto prevent him from committing himself to her as entirely as she commits herself to him. When Paolo and Francesca declare their love for each other, Paolo claims he has no regrets:

> Away with fond remorse!
> Here on the brink of ruin, we two stand;
> Lock hands with me, and brave the fearful plunge!
> Thou canst not name a terror so profound
> That I will look or falter from.
>
>   (451)

But after the affair is consummated, Paolo is filled with remorse. Too "craven" to kill himself, he wishes "For some good cause to perish in" and toys with the idea of becoming a soldier (467). In the final moments Paolo's inability to resolve the conflict between his love for Francesca and his loyalty to Lanciotto paralyzes him. Unable to defend Francesca and himself verbally and equally unable to raise his sword against Lanciotto, Paolo at last can do nothing more than passively allow Lanciotto to kill him.

Francesca da Rimini, then, does not present a simple conflict between good and evil, but a conflict in which good and evil cannot be clearly defined. From the moment Paolo and Francesca begin to understand the world around them and to recognize their love for each other, they confront choices in which right and wrong are inextricably linked. When, for example, Paolo must decide whether to describe Lanciotto to Francesca, he seems to confront a simple choice of either lying to her or telling her the truth. But to tell her the truth is to risk her judging Lanciotto by his appearance rather than by his character; at the same time, to describe his brother accurately would not be unambiguously honest. Paolo has already begun to love Francesca and she him. To tell her the truth about Lanciotto's appearance might strengthen her love for Paolo.

Unlike Boker's earlier plays, *Francesca da Rimini* does not portray noble individuals crushed by a corrupt society. The situation in *Francesca da Rimini* is not the same as that in *Anne Boleyn, Leonor de Guzman,* or *The Betrothal.* To speak of Anne as the victim of a corrupt society is possible because, whatever her earlier crimes, she is innocent of the adultery for which she is executed. Further, she achieves a dignity through her ability to confront her earlier crimes and to behave nobly in the face of her destruction. Similarly, Leonor, as well as Costanza and Juanario, are innocents struggling against corrupt worlds. It is true, as Leonor acknowledges, that her affair hurt Maria, and it is true that Costanza and Juanario triumph at Marsio's expense. But Maria and Marsio, who make only slight claims on a reader's sympathies, are corrupt characters from whom the heroes and heroines do well to escape.

In *Francesca da Rimini*, however, such is not the case. The garden in which Francesca and Paolo declare their love is no idyllic spot set apart from the deceit of their world; nor is their love a rebellion against that deceit. While the deceit of Guido and Malatesta is to some degree responsible for bringing the lovers together, the love of Paolo and Francesca does not strike at that deceit so much as it strikes at Lanciotto. For Paolo and Francesca to love, they must deceive and betray Lanciotto. But Lanciotto is not an evil force determined to wreck whatever is good and pure. Rather than a villain, Lanciotto is a man for whom both Francesca and Paolo feel a measure of love and loyalty. He, as much as they, is a victim of political intrigue; he, as much as they, struggled to behave honorably when confronted with the marriage. The tragedy of Paolo and Francesca does not lie in their being crushed by a corrupt society, but in their being torn between two noble emotions: love for each other and loyalty to Lanciotto.

These two emotions cannot be reconciled in this play, and after Francesca and Paolo make love, each tries to escape the conflict in different ways. In the scene (5.3) in which Francesca speaks of pursuing their love whatever the cost and Paolo of fleeing Rimini, Boker's point is not that one solution is more noble or heroic than the other, but that both are impossible and inadequate. Francesca's solution cannot lead to an affair which, like Leonor's transcends even as it violates conventional morality. While speaking of the cost of their love in terms of society's judgment of them, Francesca ignores that a greater cost is Paolo's betrayal of his brother.

Similarly, Paolo's desire to flee Rimini is inadequate. On the simplest level, his desire is nothing more than suicide, since he is not competent to be a soldier and hence will die in battle. And like Francesca's, Paolo's solution avoids, rather than resolves, the conflict, since to flee Rimini is to betray Francesca by denying the love he feels for her. Whatever choice the lovers make is wrong. Like Boker's earlier heroes and heroines, Francesca and Paolo are surrounded by a corrupt world. The nobility they achieve through their love, however, is bought not at the price of attacking that corruption, but at the price of betraying Lanciotto, who is himself meant to be a tragic figure.

The Tragedy of Lanciotto

Had *Francesca da Rimini* done no more than portray the tragedy of Francesca and Paolo, it would have been a successful play. But in seeking to make Lanciotto a tragic figure, the play fails. Boker of necessity had to make Lanciotto more than the conventional villain found in most treatments of the story. To have made him a Don Luis would have reduced the lovers' tragedy to a melodramatic struggle between good and evil. To avoid portraying that kind of struggle, Boker had to make Lanciotto someone for whom Paolo could feel affection; someone for whom even Francesca could feel pity.

But Boker might have made Lanciotto sympathetic without complicating his character to the point that it becomes unintelligible. From Boccaccio Boker learned of the discrepancy between Lanciotto's appearance and his sensitive nature. He sought to explore that discrepancy and to relate it to the theme of the individual and society. The problem, however, is that Boker poured as many elements as he could into Lanciotto's character without ever integrating them. Instead, these elements remain undeveloped, or are forgotten entirely, as the play proceeds. Questions about, and expectations of, Lanciotto's character are raised that the play neither answers nor fulfills; and by its end no consistent motivation informs Lanciotto's final actions.

Lanciotto and the theme of appearance and reality. Boker begins by focusing on Lanciotto's sensitive nature. The war between Ravenna and Rimini has just ended, and Lanciotto is angry with Ravenna for the havoc the war has caused. But while Lanciotto vividly describes the revenge he wishes to visit on the rival city, that desire for revenge is motivated not by a love of bloodshed but by compassion for the people of Rimini. Later, when he learns he is to marry Francesca, Lanciotto is outraged. He is aware of his deformity and fears that if his ugliness does not excite Francesca's "sidelong shuddering glances," it will elicit either "The degradation of a showy love" or pity, which Lanciotto describes as "a sting / Thrust in by kindness" (358). Troubled by the marriage, Lanciotto is willing to release Francesca from the contract. Misled into thinking she loves him, he is hurt when he learns that she does not.

Further, although Lanciotto's appearance suggests he is a man of action, he is neurotically torn between thought and action. Realizing he lacks the will to refuse the marriage, he questions whether fate or some flaw in himself makes him powerless:

Am I in the toils?
Has fate so weakened me, to work its end?
There seems a fascination in it, too—
A morbid craving to pursue a thing
Whose issue may be fatal. Would that I
Were in the wars again! These mental weeds
Grow on the surface of inactive peace.
I'm haunted by myself. Thought preys on thought.
My mind seems crowded in the hideous mould
That shaped my body.

(361–62)

More than anything else, Lanciotto fears that the marriage
will make him "A most conspicuous monster" since marrying
Francesca and assuming the role of ruler will call attention to
his deformity:

Pile Caesar's purple on me—and what then?
My hump shall shorten the imperial robe,
My leg peep out beneath the scanty hem,
My broken hip shall twist the gown awry;
And pomp, instead of dignifying me,
Shall be by me made quite ridiculous.

(362)

Lanciotto sees no solution other than suicide, and Paolo enters
as Lanciotto tries to stab himself. Claiming that he is "wretched"
over the marriage, Lanciotto describes how his sword leapt from
its scabbard and stuck in the floor surrounded by a pool of
blood, which he claims "Crawled to [his] feet, and lapped them,
like the tongues / Of angry serpents" (364). Paolo, saying that
Lanciotto has always suffered from "wild fancies," looks at the
sword and says it resembles "a blessed cross" (364). As with
the knocking at the gate in *Macbeth,* the contradictory perceptions of the sword fit the individual character's personality. But
since Lanciotto's "wild fancies" about his marriage eventually
prove well founded, Boker seems to be portraying him not as
a character with a "morbid craving" to pursue events "Whose
issue may be fatal," but as a victim of his own inability to stop
events against which "All dumb things find tongues" (363).
Having created a complex character, Boker further compli-

cates Lanciotto by suggesting that his appearance, rather than hiding nobility, mirrors a deformed personality: that, in fact, Lanciotto's appearance and reality are one. The first sight Lanciotto remembers as a child was his nurse's "husband hacked to death / By the fierce edges of these Ghibelins," and he describes how his nurse, putting her hands in the blood and making the sign of the cross three times over him, prayed that "this spot stand till Guido's dearest blood / Be mingled with [Lanciotto's]" (354). These lines do more than foreshadow Lanciotto's murder of Francesca, for his nurse's actions have affected his personality. In battle, the blood "flames on [Lanciotto's] vengeful brow" and "shrinks into [his] brain, defiling all / [His] better nature with its slaughterous lusts" (355). While Boker here recalls the "angry blot" on Caesar's brow as well as the mark of Cain, and thus foreshadows Lanciotto's murder of Paolo, he also introduces the idea that Lanciotto's nobility is threatened by a nature that is as twisted as his appearance.

That suggestion is developed toward the end of act 1, scene 3, when Paolo offers to help Lanciotto dress in order to meet Francesca. Lanciotto responds with a speech beginning "Array this lump." At first, this speech seems to show Lanciotto's awareness of his own cruelty. Telling Paolo that "some human thoughts" are "Best left imprisoned in the aching heart," Lanciotto instructs Paolo that all people, including Paolo himself, are "fouler" than they appear (364–65). "This life," he says, "Is one unending struggle to conceal / Our baseness from our fellows" (365). To Lanciotto, all people must mask their true natures and thus are "Mere slaves and alms-men to a scornful world / That takes us at our seeming" (365). At this point Paolo asks, "Say 't is true; / What do you drive at?" (365); and this question becomes the reader's, since as his speech continues, Lanciotto's meaning is not at all clear.

On the one hand, Boker has taken pains to show that Lanciotto is nobler than his appearance suggests. As a result, it would seem logical for Lanciotto to complain that he is a "slave" to his deformity, since that causes the world to miss the nobility beneath his appearance. Instead, Lanciotto asserts that whereas the world thinks him "gentle, courteous, brave"—a slightly confusing assertion in light of his earlier speeches—he is "harsh, rude, and a coward" and that his particular cowardliness is his inability "To cast [his] devils out upon the earth" and show "what a hell" the world "has forced back to canker in the heart / Of one poor cripple" (365). Now it appears that at his deepest nature Lanciotto has a "hell / Of envy, malice, cruelty, and scorn" (365); and one might logically conclude that this core of malice would cause him to work evil against the world. But neither here nor later does Lanciotto work evil, and as the scene closes, his sending Paolo to Ravenna is motivated by his fear of being mocked. Thus we return once more to Lanciotto's being a "slave" to his deformity in the sense that his deformity masks a sensitive nature. The result for the reader is that Lanciotto is becoming an incomprehensible character.

Lanciotto and the theme of the individual and society. Boker complicates Lanciotto's character still further by examining him as part of the conflict between the individual and society. Like Paolo and Francesca, Lanciotto is trapped by the machinations of Malatesta and Guido, and his desires run counter to his duty. Through Paolo and Francesca, Boker seeks to show the impossibility either of the lovers' reconciling their desires with the world around them or of escaping their conflict by fleeing the world. Through Lanciotto, he examines the question of reforming society itself as a means of resolving the conflict.

During act 3, scene 2, Lanciotto and Pepe discuss the possibility of reforming society. Pretending to mock social reformers, Pepe argues for a society "In which aspiring merit takes the lead":

> I'd have no families, no Malatesti,
> Strutting about the land, with pedigrees
> And claims bequeathed them by their ancestors;
> No fellows vaporing of their royal blood;
> No one to seize a whole inheritance,
> And rob the other children of the earth.
> By Jove! you should not know your fathers, even!
> I'd have you spring, like toadstools, from the soil—
> Mere sons of women—nothing more nor less—
> All base-born, and all equal.
>
> (405)

Asserting that he is "a very firebrand of truth," Pepe calls himself a "politician. . . . / Stirred into utterance, by some mystic power" and "itching to reform the world" (406–7). He argues that were it spread about the earth, his idea must "sprout":

> Thought never wholly dies;
> It only wants a name—a hard Greek name—
> Some few apostles, who may live on it—
> A crowd of listeners, with the average dulness
> That man possesses—and we organize;
> Spread our new doctrine, like a general plague;
> Talk of man's progress and development,
> Wrongs of society, the march of mind,
> The Devil, Doctor Faustus, and what not;
> And, lo! this pretty world turns upside down,
> All with a fool's idea!
>
> (405–6)

On the surface Pepe's speeches seem the conventional and obligatory puff for democracy found in many American plays, and because of this, critics have been led not only to accept them at face value, but also to identify Pepe as Boker's spokesman.[2] But from the play itself, as well as from Boker's other writings, it is clear that Pepe is neither an unambiguous proponent of democracy nor a spokesman for the author.

First, the character of Pepe does not support such a reading. Pepe, who here argues that people should be judged without reference to artificial distinctions, hates Lanciotto simply because Lanciotto is crippled, which is an artificial basis on which to judge a human being. In addition, Pepe hates Lanciotto because earlier in the play Lanciotto had struck Pepe for something Pepe had said in his role as a fool. Like the fools in Shakespeare, Pepe is supposed to be mentally deficient, or, as he calls himself, a "natural" (360), and this deficiency gives him license to say things others cannot say. When Pepe claims that Lanciotto has slighted "a natural man," he means not that Lanciotto has failed to recognize his inherent human worth, but that Lanciotto, who is deformed and therefore unnatural, has struck a man who is not, and further that Lanciotto has violated the social code governing the treatment of fools. As a result, Pepe plots revenge, and his speeches on democracy are part of his plot, for they are an attempt to make Lanciotto trust him. While it is possible to argue that Pepe only appears to mock democracy and that he believes his speeches, the fact remains that Pepe's hatred of Lanciotto springs more from Lanciotto's being deformed and from Lanciotto's having struck him than from Pepe's feeling thwarted because he cannot realize his inherent identity. So far as Pepe himself is concerned, he has no identity save that which society has given him.

Second, and more important, to read Pepe as Boker's spokesman ignores Lanciotto's criticism of Pepe's speeches. After Pepe describes his ideal society, Lanciotto says that those reforms will change everything except the human heart. "Man, the moral creature," will be "still unchanged; nor moves towards virtue more, / Nor comprehends the mysteries in himself" (406). Pepe replies that he cares nothing for that because he is a "politician" (406), and both Lanciotto's statement and Pepe's reply recall "Pre-eminence of the Man of Letters," in which Boker distinguished between the politician and the artist by saying that the artist wishes to change the human heart, the politician does not. Furthermore, Lanciotto associates the desire for an easy social reform with "mechanic means." "Nature," he says, "bows down to science' haughty tread, / And turns the wheel of smutty artifice" (406); and these lines look ahead to Boker's complaint in "Ad Criticum" that "Strong science strides he knows not where— / He knows not where, he knows not why."[3]

Thus, in the scene between Pepe and Lanciotto, Boker is not arguing for a democratic society as a panacea for the ills of Rimini. He is examining and rejecting yet another possible solution to the conflict his central characters confront. Through Francesca, Boker shows the impossibility of her realizing her ambitions within the existing social order; through Paolo, he shows the impossibility of fleeing that order; and through Lanciotto, he shows the impossibility of quickly reforming society. The reformation of society, if it is to come at all, must come through the reforming of the human character. In *Francesca da Rimini* Boker does not believe that society itself is the root of corruption; rather, the social order embodies the corruption inherent in the human heart. In his recognition of the source of corruption Lanciotto, not Pepe, comes closer to speaking for Boker.

Lanciotto and the theme of the wronged husband. Finally, as though Lanciotto's character were not complex enough, Boker adds yet another element. As noted before, Lanciotto first wishes to release Francesca from the marriage contract until her assertions that she wishes to marry him convince him that she loves him. In act 3, scene 2—the scene in which Lanciotto and Francesca first meet—Lanciotto becomes, as Joseph Wood Krutch describes him, a man who, always wishing to be loved, deludes himself into believing he is loved; and the play becomes "more the story of the wronged husband than of Paolo and Francesca."[4] This theme, however, lasts only through the fourth act. By the end of the act Lanciotto has discovered his delusion. He has also discovered that Ravenna has renewed the war, and at the moment when he is going to confront Francesca, he must leave for battle.

Boker's failure to sustain Lanciotto's character. By the end of the fourth act Lanciotto has been presented in the following, sometimes contradictory, ways: he is deformed, but that deformity hides a noble and sensitive nature; he is deformed, but that deformity hides a nature full of "envy, malice, cruelty, and scorn"; he is subject to "wild fancies" and attuned to the workings of fate; he is torn between thought and action; he is acutely aware of the foulness of the world, aware even that such foulness lies beneath a "Miracle of grace" like Paolo (365); he is aware that the corruption of society is the product of the human heart's own imperfection; and he is a man desperate for love and capable of being deluded.

To reconcile these elements at this point in the play is difficult. During the final act such reconciliation becomes unnecessary, since most of these elements are forgotten or, if recalled, are never integrated. Specifically, given the disparate elements of Lanciotto's character, it is difficult to find an adequate explanation for his murder of his brother. The best that can be said is that Lanciotto murders Paolo because the social code demands that he avenge the affront to his honor, and thus Lanciotto's conflict is between his adherence to a social code and his love for his brother.[5]

But while Lanciotto's speeches in act 5 focus on his honor, a concern with his honor strong enough to motivate the murder is new to the play. Earlier (4.3), when Lanciotto suspected that Francesca and Paolo were conspiring against him, it was Paolo's betrayal, not the affront to his honor, that upset Lanciotto. Later (5.2), when Pepe tries to convince Lanciotto that Paolo and Francesca are in love, it is again Paolo's betrayal that most concerns Lanciotto.

When he rushes off to find Paolo, Lanciotto says he will "stir in this business" until he finds the truth (463). The situation he discovers when he confronts Paolo and Francesca in the garden is complex, and Lanciotto has been portrayed as a subtle enough character to understand its truth. But he fails to understand; in fact, he makes little attempt at understanding. His concern in the final scene is solely his honor, and while that concern provides a convenient motivation for the murder, it fails to integrate Lanciotto's final actions with his earlier statements.

Thus themes that Lanciotto's character earlier set in motion or contributed to are forgotten. His earlier insights into fate and society's corruption; his earlier fascination with events that might prove fatal; his earlier indecision and powerlessness; his earlier statements of his own malice and cruelty; all these are forgotten. Boker is unable to sustain or to integrate the elements of Lanciotto; and at the center of the play there is only the torso of a character.

Conclusion

Despite its being the last of Boker's important plays and the only one that continues to attract attention, *Francesca da Rimini* is not Boker's most successful play. This is not to say that it is not his most interesting. Dramatically, it is far more interesting than any of the earlier plays, and Lanciotto's character, despite its flaws, is intriguing. But thematically, only the Francesca and Paolo story ranks with *Anne Boleyn* or *Leonor de Guzman*.

Considered as the tragedy of Francesca and Paolo, the play is a logical conclusion to Boker's earlier work. Francesca and Paolo face the situation Boker invoked again and again. In *Calay-*

nos he had managed almost none of the elements of his play successfully, and what was supposed to have been a tragic conclusion was nothing except a mechanically contrived spectacle. In *Anne Boleyn* Boker was able to handle his central character and to complicate her relationship with her society. So, too, Leonor's relationship with her society was subtle, and by that play Boker's understanding of his central theme had taken him a long way from *Calaynos's* simple-minded attempt to establish an ideal world.

But in neither *Anne Boleyn* nor *Leonor de Guzman* was the claim of the forces that opposed the heroines as strong or as convincing as Lanciotto's claim on both Francesca and Paolo. In this play Boker fully realized the situation he had been struggling toward from the time he wrote *Anne Boleyn:* to create an opponent who merited as much consideration and who elicited as much sympathy as the central characters. Had Boker known when to stop developing Lanciotto's character, the play might have been an unqualified success. But in his zeal to make *Francesca da Rimini* "great" Boker tried to incorporate too much into Lanciotto. From *Calaynos* on, Boker's villains had been subtle. While Lanciotto is not technically a villain, Boker tried to give him more subtlety than he had given Don Luis, Henry, Marsio, or Albuquerque. Whether any playwright might have controlled all the elements of Lanciotto is questionable; certainly, Boker could not.

Boker's failure to realize the character of Lanciotto also indicates that he had not fully overcome the technical problems of writing a romantic tragedy. While Boker is able to define Francesca and Paolo by placing them in intensely dramatic scenes, he cannot do the same with Lanciotto, whom he characterizes primarily through soliloquies. When Lanciotto must engage in a dramatic scene with another character, Boker cannot reconcile what Lanciotto does in that scene with all he has said in his soliloquies. Consequently, to motivate Lanciotto's dramatic scenes, Boker seizes upon one element of the character and forgets the rest.

The failure of Lanciotto demonstrates, then, that Boker was still hampered by the problems that contributed to the failure of *Calaynos*. At the end of that play the need for a dramatic spectacle caused the playwright to emphasize Calaynos's race, something which had been of slight importance earlier. In *Francesca da Rimini* Boker motivates the final spectacle by making Lanciotto's concern with his honor the primary element of his character. Ironically, the demands of his genre, which plagued the worst of Boker's tragedies, plagued even his best.

Chapter Four

The Late Plays and Poems

Königsmark, Nydia, and Glaucus

Written in 1853, *Francesca da Rimini* was not produced until 1855, a year before the publication of the *Plays and Poems*. Following the production of *Francesca da Rimini* and the publication of *Plays and Poems,* Boker's career changed direction as he gave up trying to achieve literary fame. The causes of that change—the relative failure of his published works, the Girard Bank lawsuit, which began in 1858, and the Civil War—have been discussed. The effects of these causes on Boker's later plays were not fortunate, since instead of continuing to develop his talent, he failed even to match the level he had achieved in *Anne Boleyn, Leonor de Guzman,* and *Francesca da Rimini.* In his early plays he had treated the heroic individual in conflict with society, and as early as *Calaynos* had not been content with portraying a simple conflict. Each successive tragedy had become increasingly complex until, with the character of Lanciotto, Boker had attempted more than he could manage. Beginning with *Königsmark* and continuing through *Nydia* and *Glaucus,* however, he simplified the issues his dramas treat. In these plays the characters have little to recommend them dramatically. And thematically the plays themselves have no depth.

Boker was working on *Königsmark* by February of 1855 and finished it in 1857. The play, which was never produced, remained unpublished until 1869, when it appeared as part of a book of poems. In addition to the play, this book included such poems as "Ad Criticum," "Countess Laura," and "The Legend of the Hounds," a sentimental retelling of a legend in which a drunken squire drives his hounds, including one who once saved his life, to their deaths. Thereupon, the squire is haunted by the hounds and eventually driven to his death. The poem treats a Pennsylvania legend, but Boker, who was never comfortable with America as a setting, changed the locale to England. The book also signalled a change from Ticknor and Fields to J. B. Lippincott as Boker's publisher.

Based on a lecture Thackeray delivered in the United States in 1855, *Königsmark* is set in the Hanoverian court of 1699 and is the story of Countess Von Platten's attempt to destroy the lives of Count Philip Königsmark—with whom she has had an affair and whom she hates for having left her—and of Sophia, wife of the future George I of England. The countess's plan, which involves a forged letter and a midnight rendezvous, is to make George think that Sophia and Philip are lovers when in fact the two are close friends whose affection, thanks to Sophia's having reformed Philip's youthful rakishness, transcends the carnal. George, however, has a suspicious nature, and to escape her husband's suspicions Sophia plans to leave the court. Using the forged letter, the countess arranges to have Sophia and Philip meet at midnight. When Philip arrives, the countess's henchman kills him. At the same moment that Sophia arrives and finds Philip dying, George arrives as well. He thinks Philip and Sophia were planning to elope, and Philip's assertion of Sophia's innocence is useless. The play ends with Philip's death and Sophia's imprisonment.

Dramatically, the play fails on two counts. First, Boker does not adequately motivate much of the action, a failure that stems from his handling of the historical material. In his earlier plays Boker often altered his sources in order to make his plays either more dramatic or complex. In *Königsmark* he takes more liberties than usual with his material, but his liberties simplify, rather than complicate, the historical material. Historically, for example, Philip and Sophia were not innocent victims, but lovers. By making them innocent, Boker has to rely on machinery to make them appear guilty, and no one, including George, should be misled by the countess's devices. Moreover, Philip does not die, as do Boker's other heroes and heroines, because he is caught up in a complex and deceitful world; instead, he is simply murdered by the countess's henchman. He is, in other words, a victim of the play's machinery, and neither his death nor Sophia's being taken to prison can be said to be tragic.

Second, the ending is, to say the least, dramatically inept. When the play ends, the audience's attention shifts from Philip to Sophia. Suddenly, she makes the chief claim on both an audience's sympathy and its curiosity. Yet Boker makes no attempt to indicate what will happen to her after her imprisonment; nor has he done much to develop her character earlier. Like Lady Alda, Sophia has little to recommend her as a dramatic character. She is innocent without, like Anne, being perceptive, and for most of the play she has nothing to do except be innocent. Lacking plausibility, the play lacks thematic interest. The good characters here are nothing other than good; the evil characters nothing other than evil; and Boker depends on his play's machinery, rather than on his characters, to direct the action.

A period of almost thirty years separates *Königsmark* from *Nydia* and *Glaucus,* and Boker's having written these last two plays was something of an accident brought about by the successful revival of *Francesca da Rimini* in 1882. *Nydia* and *Glaucus* are two versions of material from Edward Bulwer-Lytton's *The Last Days of Pompeii* (1835), and as their titles suggest, the plays differ primarily in terms of which character dominates the action. They differ as well in their endings, for Nydia, who dies at the end of her play, is alive at the end of *Glaucus.* But essentially, both treat central characters, Nydia and Glaucus, whose merit is unrecognized by the world, but who reveal that merit by triumphing over evil.

In both plays evil is represented by Arbaces, an Egyptian priest of Isis and the guardian of Ione, a beautiful and rich heiress. Ione and Glaucus, whom the world thinks a rich and foppish gentleman, are in love, but that love is threatened by Arbaces, who wishes to secure control over Ione's fortune. In addition, Ione's brother Apaecides, a neophyte priest of Isis, has discovered that Arbaces is a fraud and that the idol of Isis, a mechanical contraption worked by Arbaces' servant, is designed to bilk the faithful. Once having made that discovery, Apaecides is murdered, and Arbaces, having made it appear that Glaucus is responsible for the death, imprisons Ione in a house complete with secret passages. Although blind, Nydia knows her way through Arbaces' house, and leads Glaucus to Ione. He rescues her and, at least in *Glaucus,* all ends happily.

In *Nydia* the plot is complicated because of Nydia's love for Glaucus, which, since she is a slave, Nydia realizes can never be fulfilled. Throughout the play she suffers in silence because of her passion and reveals it only as the play is ending. By then, she herself is dying, and her death, which is meant to be tragic and moving, is merely expedient. Glaucus and Ione, both beautiful and rich members of the nobility, belong together. Were Nydia to survive, her passion for Glaucus would be excess baggage the play could never adequately incorporate. The only way for Boker to resolve the problem of Nydia is for her to die, and her death scene, which is overdrawn and sentimental, includes a sudden moment at which she can see, at least in a spiritual sense. One thing she "sees" is that it is better for her to die since there is no happiness for her in this world. But her death, unlike those of Boker's earlier heroines, is not a triumph over a complex and ambiguous world. It is instead a gratuitous resolution of an otherwise uncomfortable situation.

According to one of his notes to *Nydia,* Boker would have had Glaucus die at the play's end also, except that the plot would not allow it.[1] Thus Glaucus survives in both plays, and in *Glaucus* itself Nydia's love for him has been so weakened that she has no difficulty surviving the play's conclusion. Boker's most radical change in *Glaucus* is his development of the character of Glaucus, which is accomplished by emphasizing his apparent foppishness while at the same time indicating that Glaucus's high ideals and gentlemanly behavior make him superior to the world around him. He is not, then, like Calaynos, a multifaceted and ambiguous character, any more than is Nydia; nor is the evil the two confront anything other than deceit motivated by greed. In neither play does Boker explore his characters or his themes, and both plays are spectacle rather than drama, melodrama rather than tragedy. The weaknesses of *Königsmark* dominate *Nydia* and *Glaucus* as well, and all three late plays are a disappointing conclusion to Boker's playwrighting career.

The Later Poetry:
The Book of the Dead and *Poems of the War*

With the exception of his love sonnets, and to a lesser extent *The Book of the Dead,* Boker's poetry, whether written before or after 1856, is also disappointing. Of the poems written before 1856, the most significant are those that define his theory of poetry or enhance some of the themes of his plays (these poems have been discussed already). The other early poems are insignificant. Technically, such a poem as "The Song of the Earth," a long poem in various meters, reflects Boker's interest in prosody. But for all his concern with, and knowledge of, poetic technique, Boker was not a gifted technician. His blank verse and his sonnets, his most successful forms, are competent, but not inspired. Philosophically, such poems as "The Song of the Earth," "The Vision of the Goblet"—an ode in praise of Dionysus—and "Ode to a Mountain Oak" are trivial. For all his talk of infusing lifeless material with the fire of the imagination, Boker failed to infuse his own poetry.

Of the two books that followed the writing of *Königsmark, The Book of the Dead* is the more interesting. Written during the early years of the Girard Bank lawsuit (1858–60), it is an anomaly among Boker's works. For one thing, it does not treat his usual themes. Although Boker's portrayal of his father and himself as two noble individuals pitted against corruption recalls the situations in his plays, Boker's interest here is to defend his father's reputation, not to examine the relationship between the individual and society. In addition, the work is more intensely personal than are the plays or even the love sonnets. While Boker was not the sort ever entirely to drop what Leland described as the *"nil admirari* air" he does not disguise the profound effect the lawsuit had on him. In one poem Boker imagines that his father, viewing these events from the vantage point of heaven, regards such matters as the lawsuit as "but illusions vain."[2] For Boker himself, however, "this scene is all in all," and the emotions he expresses are real, not assumed. "I am," he tells his father, "the thing I seem to be" (19). Thus the work is a sometimes-moving account of the effects the lawsuit had on the poet.

The most obvious of these effects is outrage. Ostensibly, *The Book of the Dead* is designed to defend and restore Charles Boker's reputation. The 107 numbered poems, as well as the unnumbered prefatory poem, are meant to present an accurate account of the events surrounding the lawsuit. Yet rather than simply one document among many that will come out of the lawsuit,

Boker's book, like the Egyptian Book of the Dead, is to be
the sole document on which posterity will base its judgment:

> Beside the spreading Nile of old,
>   They buried with their worthy dead
> A scrolled papyrus, to unfold
>   His virtues and the life he led.
>
> And all the gods, in council grave,
>   Asked nothing but this written scroll,
> As evidence, to doom or save
>   The bearer's arbitrated soul.
>
>   (5)

Boker's outrage results not only from what he regards as
the inaccuracy of the charges against his father, but also from
what he sees as the betrayal those charges symbolize. By saving
the Girard Bank, Charles Boker had saved more than an institu-
tion. He had made it possible also for others to salvage their
personal and financial fortunes. Instead of loyalty, these people
repaid Boker with envy and deceit:

> The knaves who found safe shelter there,
>   Who owed him more than they could pay,
> Were eaten up with envious care
>   Because their chief was more than they.
>
> But cowards shrewd, they hid their thought,
>   And fetched and carried at his nod,
> Until his soul was upward caught
>   By the dread, sudden hand of God.
>
> In life they played their cunning parts,
>   They lauded everything he did;
> In death they—bold, heroic hearts—
>   Stabbed at him through the coffin-lid!
>
>   (8)

Moreover, ignorant of banking themselves, these enemies
based their charges on that ignorance and added slander and
"hints of guilt" until at last:

The murmur grew a general roar;
   And, in the very house he built,
They drove his children from the door.
               (9)

In addition to the outrage he directs at all the parties to the lawsuit, Boker is particularly embittered toward those who have betrayed a man who trusted and took a personal interest in them. Feeling that one such man incorporates the betrayals of both Peter and Judas, Boker devotes the eleventh poem, which is typical of the poems that express rage, to excoriating him:

Peter and Judas merged in one!
   Two traitors, matchless till thy time,
It needs to show the deed thou hast done,
   And fill the measure of thy crime.

Him thou deniedst, and sold to men,
   Was more to thee than aught on earth;
He raised thy narrow fortunes when
   The world was cold before thy worth.

Change places with that noble heart;
   If thou wert dead and wronged, would he,
I ask thee, act so vile a part
   In dealing with thy memory?

Oh, fie! conceal thy dirty gold,
   Thy secret comfort, open shame!
For thirty pieces thou hast sold
   The treasure of an honest name.

Or else let Judas' story yield
   Its fullest fruit: Take up thy pelf,
Seek out the Potter, buy his field,
   And in some corner hang thyself!
              (28–29)

But the poems do more than vent the poet's rage; they also celebrate his relationship with his father. From them it is clear that while Boker loved his father, the two did not understand each other, and one strength of the poems is that Boker does not sentimentalize the relationship. Charles Boker did not approve of his son's desire to be a poet; and George Boker did not approve of his father's single-minded dedication to business. But nothing in the record suggests that the relationship was especially stormy or acrimonious. The two simply held differing assumptions about life, and the poet seems to have understood and to have accepted that difference. In the nineteenth poem, for example, he remembers how he would try to lure his father away from the cares of business:

> Oft when thy duties bound thee down
>   To wearing labor, I, more free,
> Fled from the stagnant heat of town,
>   And sought to lure thee after me.
>
> In vain I tried the oriole's call,
>   In vain the robin's tender note,
> In vain the woodland songsters all
>   Made music in my swelling throat.
>   (40)

When nature's joys failed to entice the banker, the poet tried suggesting that working "Amidst the press and throng of men" leads to nothing but death:

> I pointed to the o'erworked dust
>   That swells the church-yard mounds: you said,
> " 'Twere better to wear out than rust:
>   There is rest enough amongst the dead."
>   (41)

Having established the two viewpoints, the poem concludes not with the poet's arguing the superiority of his view nor with an admission that the banker's view was correct. Instead, it ends with the simple recognition that father and son differed:

> Poor soul, I mourn thy labor lost;
>   Thy self-denying purpose gained,
> But gained at a prodigious cost—
>   Thy work denied, thy memory stained.

I may misjudge. Thy life to thee,
  Perhaps, was filled with joyous hours,
And seemed as fair an empery
  As that o'er which the poet towers.

'Tis for omniscient God alone
  To know who grovels, who ascends:
We work His purpose, one by one,
  In divers ways, to divers ends.

(42)

But while they had different ambitions, father and son agreed on the importance of achievement. At times, Boker considers giving over the writing of this book, particularly when he considers how little anything seems to matter in a world "That seeks no heaven and shuns no hell" (44). These feelings leave him, however, when he senses his father's presence. Curiously, then, a man who seems to have cared nothing for poetry becomes the force that impels Boker to write, and *The Book of the Dead* is motivated not only by outrage, but also by love:

I know who stands beside my chair,
  Who sternly motions to my pen;
I grasp it, in foredoomed despair,
  And ply my fearful task again.

Once more the pinions are unfurled,
  They beat the air, they mount on high,
And from this low, sin-bounded world,
  Go fanning gently up the sky.

(45)

As the twenty-third poem shows, Boker's love for his father was based on an admiration for his father's way of meeting the world. Father and son were joined by their conception of how a person should behave even while they disagreed on the specific ambitions a person should hold:

I loved thee for thy honest scorn
  Of fraud and wrong, thy tender ruth,
That touched the lowest thing forlorn,
  Thy eagle grasp on right and truth.

I never knew thy tongue to hang,
  Before rich wrong, in selfish fright;
But I have heard it when it rang,
  A clarion, on the side of right.
                                (50)

Because he did love his father, Boker naturally felt a deep
sense of loss when his father died, and that sense of loss was
compounded by the lawsuit. As a result, writing these poems
became an outlet for Boker's grief. "I can but sing," he says
in the fourth poem, "For thus one half my grief is drowned"
(15). Later, in the eighty-first poem, Boker indicates the extent
to which his grief required such an outlet:

For, lacking utterance to my woe,
  I must have writhed as one possessed,
And tossed my wild arms to and fro,
  And rent my hair, and beat my breast.

Therefore thank God that in mild song
  He still permits my pain to shroud;
And when I thunder o'er the throng,
  'Tis only from a golden cloud!
                                (166–167)

In addition to his grief, Boker's poems were an outlet for
the frustration he could not express publicly. Given the lawsuit
itself, as well as the usual way life works, Boker often met his
father's enemies in the ordinary course of a day. Like Anne
or Leonor, he sometimes found himself confronting enemies
whom he could not destroy, and he was in the frustrating position of being certain of his future victory and yet of having
to endure his enemies' present gloating. What was worse, social
convention required he feign, if not cordiality, at least forbear-
ance.

In the fifty-second poem Boker describes one such incident,
and having characterized most of his father's enemies as "The
common herd" (114), singles out four whose actions he found
most repulsive:

One fool, lob-sided and bare-browed,
  Mindless of home, in spiteful glee,
Of gibbeting my name talked loud,
  As though he shared the hangman's fee.

One blustered, swaggered, stamped, and swore,
  Till conscience was by rage beguiled;
And one, whose hair was silvered o'er,
  Babbled, unnoticed, like a child.

But all the while the subtler cur,
  Whose bark had harried on the pack,
Was out of sight; such things prefer
  To stab one's honor in the back.
                                    (115)

As the poem's concluding lines indicate, writing poetry was more than merely a way to revile such enemies. Concentrating on his poetry was also the key to his ability to retain his self-control in such situations:

And I, amidst this reptile throng,—
  Giants in fraud, but dwarfs in wit,—
Stood calmly, and composed a song,
  Like Ragner in the serpents' pit.
                                    (116)

The Book of the Dead ranges, then, across a spectrum of emotions. Considered as a sequence, it works its way from outrage and grief to a sense of victory and closes with Boker's wish that his father, whose reputation is now secure, will have a quiet rest:

The curs that brayed at thee are dumb,
  The liars strangled with their lies;
A thousand honest voices hum
  Thy praise, and not a foe replies.

No sound shall come to vex thy ears;
  Thy small domain of flowery sod

> Is hallowed, Sleep, without a fear,
> And wake but at the voice of God!
> (214)

Historically, *The Book of the Dead* is interesting for the light it sheds on the Girard lawsuit as well as on Boker's life, for it is his most autobiographical work. Like all his works, this one is uneven, and its observations on life sometimes banal:

> I do not say our journey goes
> Without some roses, there and here;
> Although short seasons has the rose,
> The thorns are growing all the year.
> (15)

Yet these poems have more power and appeal than does much of Boker's poetry and certainly have a greater sense of immediacy than does *Poems of the War.*

Poems of the War does not include every war poem Boker wrote, since in selecting the poetry for the volume he omitted such satiric poems as "The Copperhead," "Tardy George"—a satire on General George McClellan—and "The Queen Must Dance"—a satire on Mrs. Lincoln that Boker published anonymously in 1862. The poems Boker included are "serious" and "lofty." Many were based on newspaper accounts of battles; others celebrate the "cause" that justified the war; most were originally written and published as quickly as Boker could manage and appeared in newspapers or as broadsides, often shortly after the battles they recounted. When Boker was readying the volume for publication, he asked Oliver Wendell Holmes to write a prefatory piece, but Holmes, who claimed to admire Boker's poetry, declined, and Boker himself wrote an "Invocation" that stands as the first poem. He then filled out the book by adding a section of "Miscellaneous Poems."

While many American poets wrote poems inspired by the Civil War, only Whitman's and Melville's poetry continues to attract attention. For those two poets the Civil War was a national tragedy that called into question the nature of the United States. For Boker, and for most of the war poets, the war was also an event of great moment, and Boker was deeply concerned that the Union prevail. But whereas the war inspired Whitman and Melville to write significant and probing poetry, it prompted Boker to write patriotic verse that had the immediate purpose of arousing patriotism. Taking accounts of battles from newspapers, Boker versified the events of the war in the hope that those events would thereby become more real to his readers. In a sense, then, his literary method was what it had always been: to take historical material and to make it literature.

But whenever Boker wished to transform something into literature, he removed that thing from the present and forced it to fit his conception of what literature should be. Such transformation meant not only that the events had to be set to verse, but also that the diction and details had to be literary. As a result, Boker's war poems have little contact with the war they are meant to describe. They suffer from the general flaw of "popular" war poetry: namely, what they celebrate is unreal. Although Boker often makes soldiers the narrators of his poems and places the soldiers within the action, his poems fail to achieve immediacy.

For one thing, Boker's diction mars his war poems. His soldier-poets do not sing, they "troll a stave" and speak of their art as "minstrelsy."[3] For another, the words Boker uses to describe battles are often more medieval than nineteenth-century. "Pennons" are "blown out," and "Spears" slant over the soldiers (140). And finally, Boker sentimentalizes his subjects. "Before Vicksburg" describes how a young, wounded soldier struggles to reach General Sherman to ask that more ammunition be sent the troops. In the poem the young soldier is not simply young; he is "The merest child, the youngest face / Man ever saw in such a fearful place" (104). And the child is not merely wounded, but "Weeping and sorely lame" (104). "Stifling his tears" and limping to General Sherman, the child ignores the "pool" his "bright, young blood" makes "Around the circle of his little feet" until he can ask for the ammunition. Sherman, who in this poem is obtuse, will not pay attention to the lad's request, but keeps asking if the boy is not wounded. This gives the boy an opportunity to say again and again that his wounds are unimportant, but that the troops need more bullets:

> . . . the boy, toiling towards the hill's hard top,
> Turned around, and with his shrill child's cry

> Shouted, 'O, don't forget!
> We'll win the battle yet!
> But let our soldiers have some more,
> More cartridges, sir,—calibre fifty-four!"
>
> (106)

Such poetry belongs to the cult of sentiment and is meant to produce a tear, and in the poem itself Sherman is so moved he sheds a "drop" that "Angels might envy" (105).

The success with which Boker moved his readers is suggested both by the sales of *Poems of the War* and by the adulation heaped upon him.[4] Today, if Boker's war poems are thought to be no worse than similar popular poems, they cannot be considered much better. That they were based on actual events makes them no more real than if Boker had created the events. The war Boker portrays is an idealized war in which wounds, blood, and death are little more than stage properties. Far from being the real Civil War, Boker's war is the one in which Stephen Crane's Henry Fleming hoped to fight when he enlisted. To find the Civil War and an examination of its essential meaning, one must look to poets other than Boker.

The Later Poetry: Boker's Love Sonnets

The biographical background. While Boker's involvement in the Girard lawsuit resulted in a minor work and his personal concern with the Civil War in insignificant verse, his love affairs, particularly his affair with Angie King Hicks, resulted in a major work. During his career Boker wrote more than four hundred sonnets. It is not surprising that a poet devoted to established poetic forms should have been attracted to the sonnet. Yet Boker's commitment to established forms does not entirely explain the number of sonnets he wrote. Following the *Plays and Poems* and the start of the Girard lawsuit, his writing of sonnets, like his writing of *The Book of the Dead,* became a private outlet. Thus while he wrote and published sonnets on nature, a sonnet on "The Awakening of the Poetic Faculty," sonnets in memory of such people as John Sargeant, occasional sonnets addressed to Andrew Jackson and Louis Napoleon, and seven sonnets on the Crimean War, Boker devoted most of his sonnets, 371 of them, to love. Of these, however, only sixty were published in his lifetime. Although Boker at times thought of publishing the other love sonnets, they remained poems written for his "private solace, to blow off the steam of love" (LS, May 2, 1865).

The 371 love sonnets may be divided into two groups: fifty-eight published in *Plays and Poems* and 313 that form the *Sonnets: A Sequence on Profane Love,* a work which, except for two sonnets published in Leigh Hunt's *The Book of the Sonnet,* remained unpublished and unknown until 1929. Moreover, the sonnets in *Plays and Poems* and those of the *Sequence* may be further grouped on the bases of when and to whom they were written. Of the fifty-eight sonnets in *Plays and Poems* the first seven were reprinted from *The Podesta's Daughter* (1852), and two of these had appeared in *Sartain's Magazine.* The remaining fifty-one, those that first appeared in *Plays and Poems,* were written between 1852 and 1856, and some, perhaps all, were no doubt the "long string of sonnets" Boker said he wrote during the winter of 1852 (LS, May 6, 1852).

The 313 sonnets of the *Sequence on Profane Love* span thirty years (1858–87) and address three women. Of these 281 were written at fairly regular intervals between 1857 and 1871, at which later date Boker left the United States to become minister to Turkey. The *Sequence* then breaks off until June and July 1877, when Boker wrote fourteen sonnets that treat a brief affair. Finally, eighteen sonnets written between 1881 and 1887 record a third affair.

Only two of the women Boker's love sonnets address can be identified with certainty: Julia Boker and Angie King Hicks. From both external and internal evidence Boker seems to have addressed the seven sonnets in *The Podesta's Daughter* to Julia, his wife. The external evidence is simply that one of the sonnets originally published in *Sartain's* was titled "To Julia." Internally, the evidence is negative rather than positive: these sonnets do not treat themes found in the clearly adulterous sonnets.

In the seven *Podesta's Daughter* sonnets Boker protests his devotion, admires the woman's beauty, and speaks of the ennobling effects of her love. While all these themes appear in later sonnets, themes are added to the sonnets first published in *Plays and Poems* that are not found in the earlier seven. The second

of the new sonnets, "Thou who dost smile," is a seduction
poem;[5] in the sonnet "O! would that Fortune might bestow
on me," the fifth of the new sonnets, the speaker wishes for a
place "secluded from the prying world" where he, loving "beyond the prudent line," might be alone with nature and his
mistress (404); similarly, the sonnet "Your love to me appears
in doubtful signs," the sixth of the new sonnets, speaks of the
woman's "cautious action" in order to disguise her love (405)
while the next sonnet, "No gentle touches of your timid hand,"
describes the lovers' "acting [their] parts, at the harsh world's
command" (406). In these sonnets Boker treats a love that is
unmistakenly illicit, while the seven earlier sonnets contain no
hint that the lovers must hide from the world.

If the seven earlier sonnets were written to Boker's wife,
clearly the fifty-one later sonnets were not, although the identity
of the women to whom they are addressed, or even that they
address only one woman, cannot be fully determined. In December 1851 Boker, responding to Stoddard's announcement that
he was involved with a woman, wrote, "I am forever tumbling
into such things, and enjoy them as only a poet can," and he
promised to tell Stoddard of all his future affairs (LS, December
23, 1851). In January 1852, again writing to Stoddard, Boker
mentions a quarrel with his mistress, "a pretty little actress"
(LS, January 14, 1852); and in May he told Stoddard of the
"string of sonnets." Thus the woman of these sonnets may have
been an actress, perhaps one who played in his *The World a
Mask.*

By October 1852, however, Boker was involved in a new
affair (LS, October 12, 1852) that was still continuing in December (LS, December 26, 1852). But in his letters to Stoddard,
Boker does not mention another affair until February 1856.
At that time he was involved with a married woman who
"thought that she could play with edged tools, and so she picked
me up and began, but I finished the matter, as mother Nature
directs; and now the lady howls in my ears, night and day,
about her ruin, and her remorse, and her poor husband, and
Christ knows what" (LS, February 11, 1856). It is likely that
this woman was Angie King Hicks. If so, the affair with her
lasted at least until June 1864, and perhaps until December
1871. In any event, the first 281 sonnets of the *Sequence,* those
dated 1857–71, appear to address one woman, and that eighty-

six of them do address Mrs. Hicks was established by the discovery of an album in which she kept the sonnets Boker sent her.[6]

The wife of the American portrait painter Thomas Hicks, whom she married in 1855, Angie Hicks was born and lived in New York City, and Boker no doubt saw her there as well as in Philadelphia, where she often came to visit the Lelands. Following the last sonnet in her album, dated June 21, 1864, the sonnets in the *Sequence* itself treat a separation; but whether the affair itself ended in 1864 is not known. Since the sonnets in the *Sequence* that precede and follow those in Mrs. Hicks's album appear to address the same woman and since they bear dates close to those on Mrs. Hicks's copies, the conclusion follows that the entire set of 281 sonnets chronicles Boker's affair with her and that while the affair underwent a change in 1864, it lasted until 1871.

Finally, it is clear that each of the later two sets of sonnets in the *Sequence* addresses different women and that, although Mrs. Hicks was still alive when these sonnets were written, neither set addresses her. Each of the three sets of sonnets in the *Sequence* contains birthday poems—in fact, the third set of eighteen sonnets consists of little else. But the dates of the birthday sonnets do not match. In the second set the birthdate is June 28; in the third, February 26. In the first set of sonnets the birthday poems are undated, but two fall between sonnets dated October 6 and November 2; in Mrs. Hicks's album these birthday sonnets are dated October 14. Presumably this was Mrs. Hicks's birthday, but as Bradley notes, the records that would establish the date of her birth no longer exist.[7]

In short, Boker had several love affairs after he married in 1844, and he no doubt had more affairs than those for which some record exists. As he told Stoddard, he was "forever tumbling into such things," and his reputation among those who knew him is indicated by Elizabeth Stoddard's comment that Boker "could weep with his victims, but he was the sort of man that would have taken the Virgin Mary from the Ass, before Joseph, and helped her kindly into an adjoining hedge."[8] Yet, as the preceding discussion reveals, the love sonnets' usefulness as a record of the facts of Boker's life is limited.

The biographical basis of his love sonnets, particularly of the *Sequence on Profane Love,* does explain in part their lack of unity and design. At the time of the first sonnets Boker had a plan for a work whose subject would be "sexual love" and in which he would "ring all the changes upon it, in a series of poems. . . . the whole thing to be strictly subjective, with mere glimpses of the story here and there." When he originally told Elizabeth Stoddard of this plan, however, he did not intend to use the sonnet as his form. But "I shall," he said, "draw largely from my own experience" (LES, May 10, 1857).

Boker's letter to Elizabeth Stoddard further indicates that he had not yet started the work, and apparently he never did. To the extent he realized his intention of treating sexual love, he did so through his sonnets. Since they were from the start a private outlet, they were written more as the mood struck him and less as elements in a unified work. While the exigencies of his life presumably proved interesting to Boker himself, they gave rise not to a structured treatment of love, but to an uneven work that fails to sustain a reader's interest through the first 282—let alone the entire 371—sonnets.[9] Thus the sequence to Angie King Hicks neither merits, nor will it repay, being treated as a sustained literary work. Instead, its interest lies, first, in its place in the history of American poetry and, second, in its treatment of sexual love.

The sonnets' place in American poetry. Historically, Boker's sequence is the first attempt by an American poet to write a love sequence modeled at least in part on the Elizabethan sequences. Since Boker's work was unknown until 1929 and not widely read even when it was published, there can be no possibility of its having influenced such later poets as Edna St. Vincent Millay, Elinor Wylie, Conrad Aiken, Karl Shapiro, or John Berryman. But like the Elizabethans, who faced the problem of adapting Petrarchanism, these American poets had to adapt the love sequence, and Boker's love sonnets should be examined in terms of how he adapted the Elizabethan tradition.

To revive a tradition such as the sonnet sequence requires poets conscious of their art and equal to the twofold problem of renewing both the sonnet form and the sonnet's content, which includes the imagery and conventions associated with love sequences. Like Boker, Millay, Wylie, Aiken, Shapiro, and Berryman each brought an individual approach to the sonnet sequence. All possessed the necessary technical competence to work in the sonnet form, but only Shapiro and Berryman experimented with the form itself. All developed a particular tone in the sonnet, notably Millay who managed several tones ranging from intensity to a flippant, sophisticated world-weariness. In addition, Millay, Shapiro, and Berryman renewed the sonnet through their diction, writing poems that were often colloquial and idiomatic, while Berryman played with language—using adjectives as nouns, nouns as verbs—in the manner of E. E. Cummings.

Moreover, all these poets brought distinctive content to the sonnet. At one extreme, Wylie's "One Person" (1929) grew out of her obsession with Shelley, and her sonnets, marked by necrophilia and preoccupied with Shelley's decomposed body, belong to the tradition of the grotesque in American literature. Millay, especially in *Fatal Interview,* gave her sonnets thematic depth through her exploration of the inescapability, as well as the emotional cost, of love. For both Aiken—whose sonnets, like Millay's, owe much to John Donne, and whose imagery recalls that of W. B. Yeats—and Shapiro, love was a meaningful human experience that could be carried out in the face of the modern world's cynicism and sterility. And finally, Berryman's sequence focused on a violent and destructive love.

While a competent sonneteer, Boker was not an innovator in the form; nor does his technique, competent though it is, dazzle like Millay's. His career does show, however, some development in his handling of the sonnet form. Although by 1862 most of his sonnets adhere to the Italian form, his earlier ones are surprisingly flexible. Of the seven sonnets addressed to his wife, for example, only the fifth follows the strict Italian rhyme scheme and division of content into an octave and sestet. Three of the remaining six sonnets use the scheme *a b a b a b a b* in the octave, and one of these follows the Miltonic division of content; the remaining three adopt the conventional scheme for the octave, but place the turn unconventionally and are, like the sonnets first collected in *Plays and Poems,* more flexible in their division of content than are Boker's later sonnets. In the later sonnets Boker adopts the conventional scheme for the octave and limits his liberties to the placement of the turn.

In one way, Boker early adopted what became for him a standard practice in the sestet. Commenting on Robert Davidson's "Hope—A Sonnet," one of the poems Boker examined

while Hart was editor of *Sartain's,* Boker criticized the sonnet
for concluding with a couplet, which, he told Hart, "gives too
epigrammatic a turn to the last lines" (LH, March n.d., 1849).
In addition to avoiding a final couplet in his own sonnets, Boker
avoided a sestet rhymed *c d c d c d,* preferring instead *c d d c
c d,* his most common scheme, or the closely related *c d d c d
c.*

Noting a poet's rhyme schemes is useful only as a means of
measuring his awareness of a given form's possibilities, and Boker's adoption of these schemes does reveal something of his
understanding of the sonnet's possibilities, since their chief value
is the range of uses they opened for him. Aside from dividing
the sestet into three two-line groups (*c d, d c, c d* or *c d, d c, d
c*), the schemes invite a division either into two tercets (*c d d
c c d* or *c d d c d c*) or into a quatrain and two final lines which,
since they do not rhyme, avoid the "epigrammatic" quality of
a final couplet. As the sestets of two of Boker's finest sonnets
show, the scheme *c d d c c d* allowed him to handle the sestet's
sounds in a variety of ways:

> I cannot storm or fondle as a boy;
> Thought shakes his finger when my passions start
> To play the antics of a hero's part.
> I cannot make thee goddess now, now toy;
> I can but touch thee with a solemn joy,
> And fold thee gravely to my quiet heart.
>   (CXXIII)[10]

> I grant myself no fitting mate for thee,
> Thou radiant creature, gilding my dim clay
> With morning sunlight, and I cannot say
> What wrought thy miracle of love for me:
> But loving thee is nothing but to see,
> To touch, to taste, and bear the sense away.
>   (CXXIV)

Boker opens the first sestet with a clause that occupies an
entire line and then allows the couplet to stop the reflection.
Line 12 again stands syntactically alone, and in line 13 Boker
allows the repetition of the *c* rhyme to stop the poem slightly
before the cadence of the final line. In the second sestet he

plays the *c* and *d* rhymes against the onward movement of syntax, stopping the poem syntactically at the end of line 12 and then stopping it again, this time by rhyme, at the end of line 13. Noteworthy as well is Boker's manipulation of sound and cadence in these sestets through his use of parallelism, caesurae, and alliteration. As these sestets show, he was capable of managing the sonnet's resources with subtlety and skill.

Similarly, Boker could handle the sound in his octaves to good effect. His competence in the sonnet is indicated particularly by his avoiding the pauses invited by the rhymes. Ideally, an Italian octave should be unbroken, a difficult feat to manage in English with its limited rhymes. Yet at times Boker does create an unbroken octave and achieves a good effect by playing the sounds of his rhymes against the poem's syntax:

> My darling, now the slumber of the night
> Lies on thy eyelids, and thy guiltless heart
> Rocks, like an empty pinnace moored apart
> From the rough storms through which it took its flight
> To this calm haven, where the billow's might
> Dies in the swimming lily, and no start
> From life's rude outer sea breaks in to dart
> Its mortal anguish on thy sealed sight.
>
> (XXVII)

Their competence notwithstanding, Boker's sonnets, including the one just quoted, lack fire. At their worst, they are stodgy and pedestrian. Their octaves fail to catch the reader up in a complex and intense experience, and one indication of this weakness is their failure to open with memorable lines. At first glance, this might seem a trivial criticism until one considers such lines as "When to the sessions of sweet silent thought, / I summon up remembrance of things past" or "Tir'd with all these, for restful death I cry"; or, not to compare Boker only with Shakespeare, such lines as Millay's "Thou are not lovelier than lilacs,— no, / Nor honeysuckle" and "I know I am but summer to your heart, / And not the full four seasons of the year." These lines impress themselves upon a reader and compel attention in ways that Boker could not in such lines as "I have thy love, and were I drunk with joy / That were enough" (XXIII); "The

leaden eyelids of wan twilight close / Upon the sun" (XXV);
and "Roll the grand harmonies which finite mind / Can neither
reason of nor understand" (LXIV).

On the whole, Boker's sonnets also lack the excitement and
complexity found in sonnets by a poet fully able to exploit the
resources of language and imagery. In Sonnet II, which treats
the problem of the poet's sincerity, Boker writes:

> To say I love thee, is but uttering
> A worn-out phrase. The opal-breasted dove
> Coos the same story to his feathered love,
> The hills, the meadows, and the forests ring
> With various changes on the self-same string.
> In vain my fancy labors to improve
> That common utterance; for the heart will rove
> From the more complex to the simpler thing.

The problem in this octave is not so much whether the imagery
is fresh—Boker no doubt borrowed the dove from Spenser—
but whether the images have any particular appropriateness to
the subject and lend depth to his theme. In the sestet Boker
contrasts "straitened Nature" with "ostentatious Art," but the
imagery drawn from nature is never directly related to the content; nor does he try to explore the implications of his images.
He believed, as noted before, that thought and expression were
separable in poetry, and this mistaken idea did not serve him
well. While it is no doubt unfair to compare one of Boker's
sonnets with Sir Philip Sidney's "Loving in truth" or Shakespeare's "As an unperfect actor"—two sonnets concerned with
what Shakespeare calls "The perfect ceremony of love's rite"—
one has but to recall both the wit and uses of imagery of these
two poets to see the distance between what Boker attempts
and what other poets accomplish.

Thus, although competent, Boker's sonnets to Angie Hicks
make little claim on a reader through their uses of the resources
of poetry. Their interest lies instead in his handling of his themes.
In part, these themes continue those found in the plays, especially the theme of the individual's relationship with society.
To this theme, however, Boker adds the theme of sexual love,
and he casts the theme of the individual and society in terms

of the poet's relationship with society. Furthermore, unlike the plays, the sonnets do not treat characters removed from nineteenth-century America. Boker's art now becomes inextricably linked with his life. The interest in the sonnets proves, then, to be biographical—not, to be sure, as a record of Boker's external life, but as a record of the "complex case" (Sonnet I) of his internal life; and an assessment of the sonnets requires they be placed within the context of that internal life. Once that is done, it is possible to argue that, despite its inadequacies, the sequence to Angie Hicks is a radical and subtle examination of "profane love."

The theme of love and Boker's need for fame. Throughout his plays Boker focuses on two kinds of characters: those who seek to escape the world around them by creating an ideal world, and those who remain in the world but whose true and superior nature the world fails to see. At times, one character such as Calaynos incorporates both themes; at times, as with the characters of Lanciotto and Glaucus, one theme dominates. But whether embodied in one character or not, these two concerns permeate Boker's plays and reflect tensions he experienced in his life. For a variety of reasons, Boker was not at home in nineteenth-century America, and art was for him an Edenic world. His desire to be a poet was motivated in part by his wish to escape the world around him and in part by his wish to prove himself superior to that world. Yet to call himself an artist and to publish works of literature were not enough to confirm his sense of his superiority. While he disliked the contemporary world, Boker looked to that world for some confirmation of his genius and some encouragement of his ambitions. He needed fame, and he failed to achieve it.

His search for fame was foredoomed since he could have taken seriously neither of the sources from which fame might have come. The first, recognition by contemporary critics, was closed to him since America had little genuine literary criticism, if by criticism one means the informed and disinterested consideration of literature. As Stoddard realized, the critical, as well as the popular, acclaim that greeted a writer like Nathaniel Park Willis was due in large part to the lack of any rigorous critical standards, and Stoddard felt that even Longfellow had achieved his immense reputation because he had written during "the glimmering twilight of American literature in the twenties and thirties of the nineteenth century, when Bryant was the only poet and Irving the only prose writer who had attained distinction."[11] In their haste to prove America at least the cultural equal of England, American reviewers seized on anyone who could churn out something that remotely resembled literature and elevated poets like Willis and Thomas Buchanan Reed to a prominence, albeit in most cases brief, to which they could lay little genuine claim.

Like Stoddard, Boker was aware of the quality of criticism in America, and he had fewer illusions about its purpose than did Stoddard. When he reviewed other authors, Boker praised their works in the hope that such praise would help the works sell. He expected that the authors in their turn would praise his work and help it to sell. Stoddard, in his criticism, tried to apply some standards, and Boker admired Stoddard's "way of judging of even a friend's work in the abstract" (LS, October 22, 1864). But Boker felt such a course ultimately unwise. For one thing, when Stoddard criticized Taylor, Taylor was hurt; and in addition to hurting a friend, Stoddard was too ready to make literary enemies, something Boker felt would not help Stoddard's career (LS, October 12, 1860). Cynical, or perceptive, enough to see that "fault-finding strengthens the praise," Boker claimed he often included some negative criticisms in an otherwise positive review (LS, January 25, 1857). But he made no attempt to be objective in his reviews; nor did they reflect his actual judgment of other authors' works. "I hold the book-selling part of literature to be a trade—an everlasting effort to gull the public" (LS, December 26, 1852). Regarding American criticism as "a better sort of advertising—a more conspicuous sort—and that is all," Boker cared for reviews "only as they may affect the public" (LS, January 25, 1857). In *Pierre* (1852) Melville, calling the kinds of reviews that appeared in America "panegyrics," said they had a "general practical vagueness . . . without anything analytical about them." Whether or not Boker would have welcomed "analytical" criticism had he received it, he, unlike Melville, could not believe that the favorable notices he received made him "the idol of the critics."[12]

Lacking an informed criticism, America lacked as well what

James Fenimore Cooper called "an intelligent public." While Cooper argued that this public "is the best judge" of literature, he also saw that the substitution of a mass audience for an informed public resulted in "a tendency . . . to gravitate towards the common center; . . . lending value and estimation to mediocrity that are not elsewhere given."[13] Boker's attitude toward the popular success of his plays has been discussed before; given his attitude that the reading public existed in order to be gulled, popular success there, had it come, could have meant nothing. Like his attitude toward the critics, Boker's attitude toward the reading public landed him in a dilemma: the failure to recognize his greatness was proof that the public was thickheaded; but had his books sold, Boker would have had to assume either that the public had undergone a profound elevation in taste or that the public had been successfully gulled.

Inherent in the attitude of such poets as Boker, Taylor, and Stoddard toward poetry and the public lay a contradiction. Since poetry, and hence the poet, occupied a realm so far above the common herd, any attention the herd might pay poetry was proof the poet had failed to scale the heights of Parnassus. What these poets wished when they thought of recognition was that the public would acknowledge the poet's greatness and applaud him for being extraordinary while at the same time admitting its own inferiority. In his "Fitz-Greene Halleck" (1869) Taylor describes the neglect that originally greeted his subject's work and points to the recognition Halleck, who was dead at the time of the essay, was then receiving. Taylor's hope, however, is that society will change and that no longer will a poet be denied veneration in his own time. In a revealing passage Taylor speaks of a time when the public, recognizing its own limitations, will tell the poet to climb "Higher, still higher! though we may not reach you, yet in following we shall rise!"[14]

The tension between Boker's desire for fame and his disgust over striving for it is a symptom of this contradiction. Yet the number of times he returns to the subject of fame indicates the extent of his need to have his genius confirmed. To seek popularity was "to have no higher motive than vanity in the exercise of the highest function" (LS, April 26, 1851). The poet must pay no attention to his generation, but "will flourish when his generation shall have passed away forever" (LS, March

23, 1854). Boker thought Longfellow's fame proof of the age's shallowness, that no poet should "expect to be popular in an age in which Longfellow is a great poet" (LS, March 2, 1864). Nonetheless, *Plays and Poems* was "a last dash at the laurel" and when that "dash" failed, Boker complained of both the critics' and the public's having ignored him.

Unable to find confirmation of his genius through either critical or popular acceptance, Boker relied on the support of his friends. He was not the only American artist to seek such support. Throughout the letters of nineteenth-century American writers the intensity with which many of them clung to those with whom they corresponded about their art is striking. Artists, of course, work for the most part alone, but given the absence of a literary tradition and an informed audience, the American artist was not so much alone as isolated. How could an artist know if he or she in fact had ability if there were no one to confirm it? Emily Dickinson, whose isolation was far more terrible than Boker's, continued to write Thomas Wentworth Higginson (although she knew he was incapable of understanding her poetry) because she needed to ask *someone* if her poems were genuine and because, quite simply, Higginson was the only person she could ask.

During the years when Boker's hopes for a literary career were highest and were to suffer their greatest disappointment, his letters are notable for the increasing intensity with which he sought support and encouragement from Stoddard and, even more, from Taylor. "To tell you the truth," he wrote Stoddard in 1854, "I am fast losing all faith in my own genius. . . . I never had sufficient external inducement to account for the vast pile of literary lumber which I have erected, but I was kept at work by a certain dim faith in myself" (LS, September 4, 1854). Now, however, that faith was fading, and Boker told Stoddard that more than anything else he required "companionship" to achieve "a full development of [his] intellectual powers," going so far as to wish he could spend his life with both Stoddard and Taylor, whose families did share a house for a time (LS, June 11, 1855).

But Boker's letters to Stoddard never achieve the intensity of those to Taylor. Boker met Taylor in 1848 and began writing him in 1849. The relationship deepened in 1850, shortly after the death of Mary Agnew Taylor, Taylor's first wife, whom he had known since childhood and whom he had married when it was clear her death was imminent. When Mary died two months after the marriage, Boker wrote:

Dear Bayard, I wish to see you. I am unhappy about you. I have a thousand things to say to you, which I dare not write. I cannot fill the place of Mary, but, before God, I will love you, serve you, cling to you, until I rest—where she may now be sleeping. Bayard, this is no vain proffer of friendship. I never offered such feelings as these to man before—I never felt them. You are the only one to whom the secrets of my heart shall be entirely open. Will you receive me with the same confidence as I commit myself to you? (LT, December 28, 1850)

Throughout Taylor's grief, Boker continued the correspondence, discovering that he needed to share his feelings with Taylor and that a bond was being established between them:

We have both one quality of mind which smooths all things—an almost feminine tenderness for those we love. . . . Who would think this of me? who but your poor friend has discovered it in you? Is this sentiment? and are you laughing at me for making love to you, as if you were a green girl? Indeed, I do not mean it for false display. I can cry like a baby, when I think of you, alone, unhappy, companionless; and remember that you have told me how comforting my friendship is to you. (LT, January 14, 1851)

In 1852 Boker invited Stoddard to engage in a fully frank relationship. But when he wrote Stoddard, his frankest confessions were of his sexual exploits, something he did not recount to Taylor. When he wrote Taylor, Boker wrote of his doubts over his literary ability and of his affection for Taylor, and both Boker's doubts and his affection were related, since periodically he owed a rebirth of his literary ambitions to Taylor, who could convince him that he was "a man of genius, in the true sense" (LT, October 22, 1855). For Boker, the relationship with Taylor became so important that the next year he wrote, "I have loved women, dearly and tenderly, but I never loved anything human as I love you" (LT, June 11, 1856); and when Taylor left for Europe without writing Boker, Boker asked, "Have you grown tired of loving me? Am I become a burden to you?" (LT, November 6, 1856).

Boker's fears that Taylor had ceased to love him were ungrounded. Just as Boker drew strength from Taylor, so Taylor drew strength from Boker. "I can find no peace but in the shadow of your personality. You are the rock in the weary land, and thus I throw myself at your feet in all the selfishness of friendship" (LB, December 10, 1854). Each man provided the other with encouragement and emotional support, and in his sonnet dedicating *A Book of Romances, Lyrics and Songs* (1851) to Boker, Taylor described Boker as "the mate of my poetic spring" and offered him "a love to match [Boker's] own."[15]

The intensity and the terms with which Boker and Taylor expressed their affection for each other may seem curious today and might be explained by saying that men in the nineteenth century wrote one another in a conventional language which, while suspicious to us, was innocent to them. There is some truth in this argument and in the related argument that men in the nineteenth century needed emotionally intense and intimate relationships with each other because such relationships with women were impossible.

At least in part, Boker sought an intense relationship with Taylor because his attitudes toward women's intellectual abilities as well as their abilities to form meaningful relationships kept him from attempting such relationships with them. He thought the poetry written by women inferior, describing that by Alice and Phoebe Cary, two popular poets of the time, as "an uncheckable diarrhoea of filthy rhymes" (LS, January 7, 1850). Boker's assessment of the Carys is very likely accurate, yet he never subjected men's poetry, even when he did not like it, to such abuse. Further, while Boker did not think women devoid of sexual desires—"If I were the parish bull," he once told Stoddard, "I could not satisfy my modern Pasiphae" (LS, October 12, 1852)—he also told Stoddard that "the feelings of women are too shallow for my taste; and that perhaps is the reason why I never really fall in love" (LS, January 14, 1852).

Since the nineteenth century was as uncomfortable as our own with admitting that a sexual element might be part of such a male relationship, the suggestion of such an element would not only have shocked, but also surprised men like Boker and

Taylor who, living before Freud, were not as "sensitive" as we to the homosexual nuances of their relationship. Such an argument, however, incompletely explains such relationships. For one thing, the men themselves often were not as unconscious of the homoerotic element as is sometimes thought. Taylor, who seems both to have been homosexual and to have been interested in understanding his homosexuality,[16] treated the physical element in male relationships in such poems as "Hylas," such stories as "Twin Love," and such novels as *Joseph and His Friend,* in which the two central male characters hold hands, embrace, and kiss. That either Taylor or his readers could find this "innocent" is unthinkable; and when carried to extremes, the argument that the nineteenth century was unaware of, and thus untroubled by, the homosexual implications of such relationships is unconvincing.[17]

Further, there is evidence that Boker himself experienced some uneasiness when he considered too deeply his feelings for Taylor and when his letters touched on emotions he was unable to explain. But rather than trying to express these emotions, Boker said he "had better stop here than end in something which neither of us understand [*sic*] exactly, although we both feel it through and through" (LT, November 25 [?], 1852).

It is none of the present purpose to try either to define Boker's sexuality or to offer a simple psychological explanation for the sonnets to Angie Hicks. There is no evidence that Boker had the same sexual feelings as did Taylor, and there is overwhelming historical evidence that Taylor was not the Dark Lady of Boker's sonnets.[18] Nevertheless, Boker wanted an intense and intimate relationship with Taylor, one requirement of which was that Taylor confirm and strengthen Boker's belief in his genius and one drawback of which was the tension in which Boker found himself. But whether he consciously entertained sexual feelings for Taylor is both impossible to determine and irrelevant.

What is relevant to a reading of the sonnet sequence is the situation that confronted Boker around 1857: the disappointing results of his literary career, his father's death and the onset of the lawsuit, and the complex relationship with Taylor that was strongest between 1850 and 1856. The first two of these forces made Boker an increasingly private poet, and he turned his attention to his love sonnets. But in writing these sonnets, Boker could no longer believe he would enjoy critical or popular success. Nor after 1857 did he look to Taylor for the same encouragement and support he had earlier sought. Instead, that support came from Angie Hicks. Again, except from the sonnets themselves, it is as impossible to determine what Boker "really" thought of his mistress as it is to determine from his letters what he "really" thought of Taylor. But in the sonnets Boker treats a relationship with a woman that took the place of the relationship with Taylor, finding confirmation of his superiority to the world around him in his love for Angie Hicks and in her acceptance of him. Most important, Boker makes his sexual relationship with his mistress an essential element of that superiority.

The nature of love.   Boker's substitution of his love affair for his earlier search for poetic fame takes place in the sixteenth sonnet. Confronted by "All the world's malice, all the spite of fate," Boker argues that both of these are powerless against love:

> Thus to the wind I cast
> The poet's laurel, and before their date
> Summon the direst terrors of my doom:
> For with the myrtle symbol of my love,
> I reign exultant, and am fixed above
> The petty fates that other joys consume.
> As on a flowery path through life I'll move;
> As through an arch of triumph pass the tomb.

In making this substitution, however, Boker is not giving up being a poet; rather he is conceding the arena in which his poetic ambitions will be carried out and the terms in which they will be fulfilled. In exchanging the laurel for the myrtle—a line that recalls Wordsworth's description of Dante's sonnets—Boker is choosing the sonnet rather than the drama. But as the seventeenth sonnet shows, the role of poet-lover requires a superior human being willing to risk "These awful joys," since in risking them the poet chances both society's disapproval and heaven's condemnation. Faced with the option either of denying his "essence" by living conventionally or of releasing that "essence," Boker asserts that either he "must die, or here become a god."

As suggested by the play on "die" and on the releasing of one's "essence," the wit in Boker's sonnets is largely sexual. From one point of view, to die or to become a god means either to live conventionally, and hence to die in a figurative sense by denying one's true identity, or to live unconventionally and hence heroically. From another perspective, however, to die refers, as in some of Donne's poems, to the loss of tumescence following intercourse. Thus in Boker's sonnet to become a god also means to perform sexually; and to release one's essence means both that the poet's true and unconventional nature is freed and that the poet has an orgasm.

Similarly, in sonnet XLII Boker returns to this sexual wit. He imagines that were his mistress to "give [him] . . . / The virgin treasure of her modest love," the result would be "A rapture" the "gods above" would "Envy." But Boker also imagines himself unable to be godlike, since exhaustion would inhibit his sexual performance:

> Yet at that weakness I would fret and pine
> Which makes exhausted nature trip and fall
> Just at the point where it becomes divine.

The function of Boker's wit is to show the impossibility of separating spiritual and physical love. At times, Boker portrays an ideal, which is to say a nonsexual, woman and is disgusted by his own corruption, which is to say his sexuality. In sonnet LXX, for example, Boker contrasts the woman's "distaste" for sex with his own "brutish thirst." Although his mistress "calmly puts aside / Her own distaste" (LXX), Boker is "ashamed" of "The passion" that makes him "Deface her virgin temple" and "foully roll / In orgies that pollute the sacred bowl" (LXXI). Yet as the very next sonnet shows, to escape sexuality is impossible. Trying to imagine himself able to "grow in some remote degree / Nearer to the whiteness of [his] darling's love" and thereby to become able to approach "those lights above" that shine through her eyes, Boker finds that

the vision of those eyes
Awakes the fiery current in [his] veins
With longings wild, mixed thrills of joys and pains;
Remembered kisses, burning with the dyes
That flushed her cheeks, the struggle, sobs and sighs,
Ere her chaste will lay vanquished in my chains.
                                                    (LXXII)

Placed in the context of the entire sequence, this sonnet's
final images are designed not so much to define sexuality's only
effect on a relationship as to define a possible effect. While
sexual love can lead to the woman's degradation and, conversely,
the man's as well, it is also potentially ennobling. Like the lovers
in his plays, Boker and his mistress must move in the actual
world; and in addition to making them superior to that world,
their love creates an ideal world. Risking the disapproval of
both society and heaven, the lovers are willing to take such
risks since love is "heaven attained" (XXXI). If there is a
heaven, Boker tells his mistress, and if he ultimately goes there,
he will find it "pervaded by a sense of [her]" (LIV).

To enjoy a sexual relationship now is "to rob heaven of all
its promised charms," since the woman is herself a heaven.
As a result, Boker finds his heaven "within [her] arms"
(LXXXVIII); and whatever the risk, love is the best guide to
heaven, for while engaging in love, one is "gazing in God's
greeting face" (CLXXX). Moreover, love is "In every giving,
/ . . . like Christ's [love], embracing all" (CCXXXIX).
Through their love, the lovers create an "Eden" (CCLIV), a
heaven on earth that makes them cling to life (CIX,
CCXXXVIII) because love is an embodiment here and now
of a future heaven.

Boker's argument that love is a guide to a higher reality
may appear platonic. But rather than an initial element to be
given up as one ascends to a higher reality, sexuality remains
essential for Boker; indeed, sexual love is the source of that
higher reality. This is not to say that sexual love in itself is
synonymous with a higher reality; rather, the quality of the
sexual love determines whether the lovers are degraded or enno-
bled by their experience.

In sonnet XLV Boker contrasts the sexuality of his present affair with that of his earlier affairs. Portraying himself as Odysseus wandering "With wanton Circe and her bestial kin," he describes his earlier life as "a wilderness of love" in which he sacrificed "Each proffered heart to suit [his] fickle ways"; and significantly, Boker does not suggest simply that his earlier mistresses made him a beast, but that he in turn was responsible for their degradation. What separates his present affair from his earlier experiences is that rather than "love's toy," he has now established a relationship with a "mistress of [his] soul" (LXXIV); and as already seen, this love of two souls retains, rather than foregoes, sexual love.

Sexual love, then, creates a new Eden, and to divorce the ideal and the sexual is impossible since the two are one. When the woman is physically absent, Boker's love, unlike Donne's, does not enjoy "an expansion." Instead, when the woman is absent, so too is the love (LXXVIII). The two kinds of love are present only when the lovers are together. When the lovers enter the Eden of sexuality, they enter the realm of both the body and the soul. In this realm sexual passion is "holy love," and "all that follows" the initial desires—"The fervid kiss, the interlocked caress— / Is heavenly pure to love's most dainty sense" (CCLXIII).

Such love transforms the poet and leads in the fiftieth sonnet to an almost Whitmanesque discovery of self—soul and body. While Boker does not catalog the parts of his body as completely, explicitly, or with as much abandon as Whitman, he writes of his renewed "self-esteem" and of touching himself "with reverence." The love has made him "A something set apart from all things near," something above "the pollution of the common stream"; the woman, "whose gracious breath has blown / This bubble in [his] spirit," is similarly transformed. Like the poet, she is both a spiritual and a physical being whom Boker describes as such a mixture of "charm" and "religion's fairest grace, / That love and worship struggle endlessly" (CCLXXI). Recognizing the impossibility of separating the "charm" and the "grace," Boker's sequence accepts and celebrates the physical and the spiritual.

For Boker, the ability to arrive at this perception and to risk

the "awful joys" of the relationship separates him from the
world around him and inspires his literature, specifically these
sonnets. Yet he still requires confirmation of his genius—in
other words, some kind of an audience who by accepting his
work will allow him to believe in his own greatness. In part,
his mistress's function is to be that audience.

Of all the love conventions, one of the most common is the
poet's assertion of his sincerity. As indicated earlier, Boker did
not bring a great deal of wit and skill to his sonnets that treat
this convention, but he did make his argument of sincerity thematically important, for the woman's belief in his sincerity is
essential to his believing his genius has been confirmed. By
accepting the "worn-out phrase" (II) and the poet's "prattling,"
by accepting his "platitudes . . . / The same weak things repeated o'er and o'er," the woman is "gracious" and confirms
the poet's worth because "those words again / Each time she
hears more kindly than before" (CCLXXV).

Feeling that his earlier poetry has been judged "rhymes of
common worth" that had "an easy birth, / And scanty night
in favor to remain," Boker admits his earlier ambitions may
have been futile:

> I grant it may be I have sung in vain,
> Scattered my seed about the barren earth,
> Sowed for a harvest where I reaped but dearth,
> And won for fee man's tolerant disdain.
> As I declare it, so the thing has been:
> Mild praise, dim glory, these have been my cheer
> And best return through many a toilsome year.

Nonetheless, Boker feels that his mistress's acceptance of his
poetry insures his having achieved a poetic crown:

> Yet when unnoticed I forsake this scene,
> Shall I die wholly? Shall no spray of green
> Start from my dust beneath thy sacred tear?
>   (CXLVIII)

But while the sonnets met Boker's needs both to transcend
his time and simultaneously to find confirmation of his superiority, one problem remained: the lovers' separation. In 1864,

when the sonnets indicate that the lovers separated, Boker treats the problem by asserting that the sonnets are a substitute for their being physically together.

Sonnet CXXXII, the first of several to treat the theme of separation, argues that being apart is yet another test of the lovers' superiority:

> Love has no triumph and no future crown
> For feeble hearts, that cannot stand the test
> Of adverse fortunes—trials wellnigh blest,
> Since through his strength we tread opponents down.
> The heart that shudders when a blast is blown,
> And beats in wild despair its helpless breast,
> The May-day reveller who pants for rest
> At sunset, Love forever will disown.

When their love began, they "danced in riot." At its noon they "worshipped Love with rites that seemed like play." Now they must become more serious, their love more mature:

> But see, our evening is already gone,
> And darkness filters downward through the gray!
> We must draw closer as our night comes on.

In the next sonnet Boker asserts that although the lovers "in the body . . . divided stand," they must "draw closer . . . in the soul" (CXXXIII). That the sonnets are the means by which the lovers can accomplish this becomes clear in Sonnet CXXXIV:

> They cannot part us. With this power of song,
> Through every circumstance, and time and place,
> I hold communion with thee face to face,
> And baffle thus the eyes that round thee throng.

Boker than asserts, in lines that recall Wyatt's speech before Anne's death, that the sonnets will contain hidden meanings inspired by his mistress and comprehensible only to her. Thus the poetry will continue to reveal the poet to his mistress and will connect the lovers spiritually, if not physically:

In every verse of mine that shines among
The printed rubbish of this age, thou'lt trace
Some hint to thee, some line that wears a grace
Which to thee only can by right belong.
Though they encase thee in a tower of steel,
My subtle spirit shall break through the bars,
And in thy presence its old form reveal.
This lute shall tinkle underneath the stars,
While others sleep; and thou shalt hear and feel
Love's voice in sounds that rattle with the wars.

The poem's argument assumes that the mistress will read the poet's published poetry, and Boker, who was not publishing much at this time except for the war poems, was too discreet to consider publishing his love sonnets. Moreover, in the sonnets themselves he had already indicated that to separate love into its spiritual and physical aspects was impossible. Thus two sonnets later he admits that the sonnets cannot take the place of his lover's presence:

Except these flights of song, I nothing have,
As consolation for thy absence, Dear;
Nothing to stop the wanderings of the tear
That still my troubled countenance will lave.
But what device, however strong and brave,
Strings up my soul against besieging fear,
Like thy light laugh, as welcome and as clear
As summer sunlight to the purblind slave?
What line as soft as thy bewildering hand
Touching and fleeing? What imagined good
Can fill the vacant place where thou hast stood?
What fancy reach, and for an instant, stand
Upon that summit where my dizzy blood
Rose to thy kiss, and answered its demand?
                                              (CXXXVI)

In 1871 the lovers suffered a serious separation when Boker entered diplomatic service, and there was no longer any way for him to pretend the sonnets could take the place of their being together. The poet cannot pretend the "lute" is his lady "nestling o'er [his] heart" (CCLXXX). "Hollow wood and tinkling wire" are powerless to disguise her absence, and the poet cannot find warmth "at a painted fire" since the physical separation marks the end of the stimulus necessary to sustain both the love and the art. "Fancies" must replace actualities, and the sequence to Angie Hicks concludes with the poet's despair over having "To guess from shadows what the substance meant; / To live on shows and seemings," and to "smile on ills that almost send / Love to the cloister of the penitent" (CCLXXXII).

The sonnets to Angie King Hicks reveal the course Boker took when he gave up a public literary career. They were indeed a private outlet that fulfilled several of his emotional needs. The affair became a source of his art because the affair provided him with both a subject and an impetus to write. The sonnets became a means whereby Boker could sustain his belief in his own genius and hence in his own superiority, while his mistress's acceptance of his poetry became a substitute for fame. Most significant, the sonnets became a vehicle through which Boker examined the nature of a sexual and an illicit love. Though the sonnets' style is old-fashioned, and though they do not quite succeed as vibrant poetry, they remain in their own way one of the most radical and interesting works of nineteenth-century American poetry. They also salvage what otherwise would have been an entirely disappointing conclusion to Boker's literary career.

Chapter Five

The Frustration of Boker's Literary Career

Boker's literary career was for him a series of frustrations. Financially secure, he did not worry about whether his writing could support his family; nor, at least early in his career, did he need to trouble himself with finding time to write. From the beginning he possessed the two things, money and time, for which many writers struggle. Gifted as well with a striking appearance and social grace, Boker had no difficulty making the contacts that assist a literary career. He moved in the same social circles as editors and publishers, and he easily met and befriended a prominent writer like Bayard Taylor, who could arrange for the leading publisher of the time, Ticknor and Fields, to publish *Plays and Poems*. When, in later life, Boker sought yet another publisher, he could turn to another of his friends, J. B. Lippincott. While his background was not as intellectually or as socially sophisticated as that enjoyed by Henry James, he was born to a situation many writers would have envied.

Yet Boker's dream eluded him. In spite of his advantages he never realized his ambition of becoming a preeminent man of letters. He blamed his failure on two causes: the events that, beginning with his father's death in 1858 and the subsequent lawsuit with the Girard Bank, disrupted his career; and, second, the little encouragement he felt he had received between 1848 and 1856. Certainly, the lawsuit, the Civil War, and Boker's diplomatic service took time away from his writing. But his career probably would have ended after 1856 even without these events.

By 1856 Boker had after all tried everything he could think of to achieve some measure of recognition: he had published his plays as soon after their completion as possible; he had tried to get them staged, often to find that no one could handle the roles; he had tried writing directly for the stage, but had found the popularity it brought not worth the cost; in desperation, he had published *The Podesta's Daughter* to regain some measure of self-respect, but that book had failed to sell; and claiming he wanted to leave his literary models behind and strike out in his own direction, he had returned in *Leonor de Guzman* to the only kind of work he could do and had followed that play with what he hoped would be a "great triumph." But the stage success of *Francesca da Rimini* was not the kind of triumph for which Boker hoped. The "great triumph" would have been the success of *Plays and Poems.* When that book failed, Boker's ambition also began to fail.

Throughout his career Boker had written quickly, completing a play within a few months or weeks and following one play with another in the space of a year or less. After *Francesca da Rimini,* however, he took two years to complete *Königsmark,* and the length of time indicates the waning of his ambition. He could no longer convince himself that the pursuit of literature was worthwhile. As Boker saw it, a possibly brilliant career had amounted to little more than one frustration after another.

A critic sympathetic to Boker also sees that career as a source of frustration. But whereas Boker saw work after work greeted with indifference, a critic sees work after work fail to prove entirely satisfactory. Though not a genius, Boker obviously had considerable intelligence and ability; yet he always remains on the verge of doing something unequivocally significant. Each of the early tragedies is better than the preceding; *Francesca da Rimini* attempts more than does *Leonor de Guzman;* the sonnets to Angie Hicks continue and deepen Boker's exploration of his themes. Yet each work remains unsatisfactory, and that failure results in part from Boker's never having found a literary method adequate for his intentions. Thus an assessment of his failure requires an assessment of his method in terms of its relationship to both the history of romantic drama and the history of the romance in America.

Boker and Romantic Drama

During his career Boker made a number of unfortunate choices, beginning with his decision to be a playwright as well as a poet. As a writer of plays he hoped would be produced, Boker had the misfortune of writing at a time when the standards of the theater were not high and originality was not encouraged. The central weakness of the nineteenth-century theater in both England and America was that no one person was expected to possess all the skills necessary to make it both financially and artistically successful. Shakespeare, a playwright, an actor, as well as a theater manager and owner, understood all the facets of his profession. Some nineteenth-century playwrights did not even understand how to construct a play that was stageworthy.

In the nineteenth century the theater was fragmented. Actors formed one group and wanted certain kinds of material that would insure their success. Owners and managers, who were sometimes actors as well, monitored public taste and sought a product that would have the widest appeal. Playwrights such as Boker were literary men who, holding themselves aloof from the practical concerns of the theater, regarded the theater-going public with disdain. Consequently, each group had different aims and was speaking a different language. When the theater in Europe did regain its position as an important literary force, it did so through the works of such playwrights as Ibsen, who came out of the theater, understood its potential, and had the facilities to stage innovative dramas. Had Boker's ambitions included writing innovative dramas, he could not have had them staged. He did not recognize, however, that the restrictions of the theater made it impossible for him to realize the literary ambitions he did have.

When Boker decided to write plays, he found his options limited to comedy, melodrama, or romantic tragedy. Like any writer with literary aspirations, Boker chose tragedy, failing to see that this genre would never adequately express the complexity of his themes. He correctly felt that character should give rise to action. But though romantic tragedy required one kind of action, Boker's characters often required another. His intention was to dramatize universal human truth, and the demands of his genre pull against that intention. In both *Calaynos* and *Francesca da Rimini,* for example, he reaches a point where his characters, Calaynos and Lanciotto, have become both complex and fascinating. In both plays, however, Boker cannot maintain that complexity since his genre demands a final spectacle. Unfortunately, the truth these two characters represent cannot be revealed through spectacle.

In addition to demanding certain kinds of action, romantic tragedy also imposed the necessity of treating historical or legendary material whose plots were fixed, and Boker did not recognize that treating fixed material was another obstacle to fulfilling his intentions. This problem is most acute in *Francesca da Rimini*. Had Boker wished to do no more than dramatize existing material, the Francesca story would have been an excellent choice. Boker, however, did not intend his plays to be mere dramatizations. To his credit, he always sought to explore the nuances in his material, and he thought he had found an important nuance in the Francesca story when he made Lanciotto a character for whom the audience can feel sympathy.

The obvious thing would have been to forget history, Dante, and Boccaccio and to write a play about a seemingly insensitive man who finds that his brother appears to betray him. That would have required that Boker rely on his own ability to create the plot. Rather than do that, he tried to force his conception of the Francesca material onto situations whose outcome was established. No matter how much he might change and complicate Lanciotto, Lanciotto must at some point murder Paolo and Francesca. Thus at the end of the play, when Boker's sources demand a particular action from Lanciotto, Boker's transformation of the character no longer fits that demand. Unable to alter the historical and literary records, Boker must simplfy his portrayal of Lanciotto. Once more, his intentions and his literary method conflict.

For Boker, one attraction of romantic tragedy was that it seemed to place him within a great literary tradition that reached back to Shakespeare. But the influence of Shakespeare, or at least the way in which Boker handled that influence, proves a further obstacle to his fulfilling his intentions. Essentially, the problem is that he borrowed from Shakespeare without ever making those borrowings purposeful. Fortunately, while all of Boker's plays are influenced by one or another of Shakespeare's plays, that influence is often superficial enough to be ignored. Such is not the case, however, with *Francesca da Rimini*, where Lanciotto's character is nothing more than a concoction of Shakespearean heroes.

When he first appears, Lanciotto recalls Shakespeare's Richard III. His appearance is similar to Richard's, and his soliloquy beginning "I, the great twisted monster of the wars" (357) echoes Richard's "I, that am rudely stamped" (1.2.16).[1] At first, Boker seems to move beyond merely echoing Shakespeare, since while Lanciotto's appearance and speeches recall Richard, Lanciotto's sensitivity toward his deformity and his concern for his people do not. But as the play proceeds, Boker complicates Lanciotto's character not by refining and deepening it, but by adding further Shakespearean elements to it. In his soliloquy in act 1, scene 3, Lanciotto begins to sound like Hamlet. Lanciotto's line "To sweat and toil under the world's broad eye (362) recalls Hamlet's "To grunt and sweat under a weary life" (3.1.77); and Lanciotto's meditation on suicide, his indecision, and his feeling that thinking saps his ability to act further recall Hamlet.

Immediately, however, Boker seems to be modeling Lanciotto on both Julius Caesar and Macbeth. The echoes of *Julius Caesar* begin when Lanciotto worries over the portents that seem to warn him against marrying Francesca:

> Why do these prodigies environ me?
> In ancient Rome, the words a fool might drop,
> From the confusion of his vagrant thoughts,
> Were held as omens, prophecies; and men
> Who made earth tremble with majestic deeds,
> Trembled themselves at fortune's lightest threat.
>   (361)

The echoes of *Caesar* quickly end with Lanciotto's description of the mark on his forehead, which, as noted before, recalls "The angry blot" on Caesar's brow. Once Lanciotto begins to wonder whether fate is leading him to his destruction, once Boker introduces the device of the sword to embody his character's inner turmoil, the play resembles *Macbeth,* since for a few moments, Lanciotto, like Macbeth, appears to be a victim of his inability to resist the machinery of fate.

In the very same scene Boker decides to borrow from *King Lear.* When Lanciotto instructs Paolo that all people are "fouler" than they appear, he concludes by saying

> Here stands one
> In vestal whiteness with a lecher's lust;—
> There sits a judge, holding the law's scales in hands
> That itch to take the bribe he dare not touch;—
> Here goes a priest with heavenward eyes, whose soul
> Is Satan's council chamber.
>
> (365)

In their perception of hypocrisy, these lines recall Lear's

> Thou rascal beadle, hold thy bloody hand!
> Why dost thou lash that whore? Strip thy own back;
> Thou hotly lusts to use her in that kind
> For which thou whip'st her.
>
> (4.6.164–67)

Like Lear, Lanciotto sees and is disgusted by the foulness lying beneath appearance. But Boker makes little of Lanciotto's perception; and when the play becomes that of "the wronged husband," Boker allows Lanciotto to play Othello to Pepe's mundane Iago.

The problem with Lanciotto's character is not the presence of these elements. At no point is Boker "copying" Shakespeare by trying to create another Richard, Hamlet, Caesar, Macbeth, Lear, or Othello. The problem lies instead in Boker's failure to see that the various elements he borrows cannot be reconciled either with one another or with the demands of the play's action. The borrowings never coalesce into a consistent character. The Shakespearean elements remain borrowed; they never become Boker's.

In terms of thematic complexity and dramatic power *Francesca da Rimini* is the climactic point in Boker's career. It is also the moment when the problems inherent in his literary method reached their own climax. The demands of romantic drama for certain kinds of action, the demand that Boker treat historical or literary material, and the influence of Shakespeare proved insurmountable when Boker tried to bring his own insight to the Francesca story. The frustration lies in watching as his intentions are thwarted by his method, a method that causes the play to end in the thematic confusion of a final scene which, if possible, is worse than the last scene of *Calaynos*. When Boker took up his next play, *Königsmark,* the problems of method remained; and as in *Nydia* and *Glaucus,* his only attempt to solve those problems was to simplify his intentions.

Boker's literary method imposed still another problem for him: the requirement that he imitate the style of Shakespeare. Boker's style is a barrier to an enjoyment of his works not simply because the style is sometimes inept, but also because it is inappropriate. His style is also symptomatic of a larger problem in his works: their relationship, or lack of one, with their own time. As Emerson knew, the style of a literary work needs some connection with the time in which it is written. In his journal Emerson warned himself not to write "modern antiques," but to recognize that an author "may well take an ancient subject where the form is incidental merely, like Shakespeare's plays, and the treatment is simple, and most modern."[2] Boker mistook the "incidental" for the essential and exaggerated the importance of what Emerson called the "costume."[3]

When Boker invoked Shakespeare to justify the style of his works, he missed the most obvious thing about Shakespeare. Rather than separable from his own time, Shakespeare belongs unmistakably to his time, so much so that for many readers Shakespeare is synonymous with his age. Boker did not grasp the paradox of "timeless" art. Dante, Shakespeare, Milton, Michaelangelo—all these artists belonged to their respective ages before they became, for later generations, "timeless." To understand any one of these artists apart from his age is impossible. They did not stand outside their time; they were part of their time. By adopting a style of writing which he thought would make his works "timeless," Boker succeeded only in making them anachronistic.

Boker and the Romance in America

Boker's literary method—his choice of romantic drama, his choice of subject matter, and his reliance on Shakespeare—represented an attempt to escape his age, an attempt to follow the famous advice he gave Richard Stoddard. In "Ad Criticum" Boker argued that, like Shakespeare, he was setting his works in a universal time and place and that, by escaping the present, was selecting material more suggestive and richer in its implications than anything to be found in the everyday world of nine-teenth-century America. Seeking that richer world, Boker chose not to treat American subjects, but to discover the material of literature in other times and places.

In the nineteenth century the issue of whether an American writer should treat American subjects was a mixture of patriotism and literary theory, and even in the twentieth century the patri-otic element of the issue survives. Arthur Hobson Quinn titled his early essay on Boker "George Henry Boker, Playwright and Patriot," and Edward Bradley adopted much the same terms when he titled his biography *George Henry Boker, Poet and Patriot.* But Boker's decision not to treat American subjects is not an occasion for assessing his patriotism; it is an occasion for assessing his place in the history of the romance in America.

Today, discussions of the romance in America inevitably begin with Hawthorne. Like Boker, Hawthorne felt the contemporary American scene lacked an "atmosphere" essential to the literary imagination. There was in America no "Faery Land, so like the real world, . . . but with an atmosphere of strange enchantment."[4] As Boker said in "Ad Criticum," America lacked suggestiveness (an idea also expressed by Taylor when he wrote that "the destiny that placed us on this soil robbed us of the magic of tradition, the wealth of romance").[5] For his part, Hawthorne adopted the romance as a way "to establish a theatre a little removed from the highway of ordinary travel."[6] By doing so, Hawthorne hoped to escape the novelist's commit-ment to "a very minute fidelity, not merely to the possible, but to the probable and ordinary course of man's experience"[7] and to achieve the "improved effects" possible in romance.[8] Hawthorne, like Boker, wished to examine a situation and to find its essential meaning; and the romance made it possible to carry out "a far more subtile" exploration.[9]

Although plays rather than works of fiction, Boker's works represent an attempt to escape the limitations of the actual, and their settings are designed to afford the writer an opportu-nity to explore the essential truths of human experience. History, as Boker told William Gilmore Simms, provided a framework in which the poet could exercise his imagination. By adopting the romantic drama, Boker freed himself from having to create settings and characters that closely approximate the "real" world. His settings become symbolic landscapes. His characters move in castles, gardens, and cities that are representative of moral realities. His interests, like those of Hawthorne, were the internal experiences of his characters. To a certain extent the machinery of romantic drama—its suggestive settings and indeterminate time, its larger-than-life characters, and their extreme passion, guilt, and conflict—provided him with the means to explore the issues that were for him most important.

Yet the romance held other attractions for writers, and in his discussion of "The Romantic in Literature and Art" Charles Godfrey Leland, Boker's close friend, focuses on them. Leland argues that romance became an important element of art in the Middle Ages. Thanks to Christianity, men were able to see the world correctly and to recognize it as a place of romantic beauty. Romance, which according to Leland is a longing for the suggestive and mysterious, creates a heightened sensibility attuned to the beauty inherent even in ugliness. Consequently, romance "is better adapted to the present complex state of society than the strictly classical" because the "romantic faculty" better enables us to see the unity of the good, the beautiful, and the true.[10] Romance, Leland concludes, takes us out of, and makes us insensible to, our dull world.

Several differences exist between Hawthorne's and Leland's theories. First, Hawthorne speaks specifically about fiction and is seeking to define a literary form based on a theory of the imagination. Leland, on the other hand, speaks more generally and by contrasting the romance—and the romantic—with the classical, emphasizes a general effect found in various art forms. Second, while both Hawthorne and Leland discuss romance as a suggestive art that leaves the present and expands the realm of possibility, the "romantic faculty," as Leland interprets it, makes us insensible to our world. Although he begins by saying that Christianity allowed mankind to see the world aright and thus initiated romance, Leland never establishes a connection between the world as it is and the world as seen through romance. Inherent in Leland's discussion is the idea of literature, or art in general, as an escape into the exotic, whereas for Hawthorne the romance is "a neutral territory, somewhere between the real world and fairy-land, where the Actual and the Imaginary may meet, and each imbue itself with the nature of the other."[11]

Thus while Hawthorne regards romance as a merging of the actual and the imaginary, Leland views it as an escape from the actual altogether. Within the history of American fiction, this difference forms the basis of Richard Chase's division of American romancers into two groups, the first of which includes such major figures as Hawthorne and Melville, the second of which encompasses such writers as Lew Wallace and Margaret Mitchell.[12] For the writers in the first group the romance provided a method through which the reality beneath the world's surface could be known; for the second group it provided an escape from any kind of reality at all. In other words, the devices of romance—the subject matter, characters, settings, actions, props—can be suggestive in one of two ways. While such devices may provide a writer with a springboard to a more complex and a more real realm than the actual, they may also provide a writer with nothing more than the means of evoking easy, and ultimately false, emotional responses.

Boker is too complex an artist to be placed entirely in Chase's second group. At his best, Boker succeeded in using the devices of romance as vehicles for examining significant human issues. The scope of his thematic interests was not large. He concentrated on how individuals react to a world that fails to satisfy all their desires or ambitions, and his approach to his theme was conservative. Through his villains, Boker examined and rejected the idea that the individual's highest duty is self-fulfillment; and he rejected this idea not so much because he thought it immoral, but because he thought it failed to deal adequately with the reality of human experience. For him, any individual desire had to be assessed and modified in terms of its relationship to the individual's responsibility to others. For Anne and Leonor in Boker's plays, this responsibility required that they examine the effects of their actions on society at large. Both had to recognize that their ambitions could throw their respective nations into chaos, and both sacrificed their desires rather than cause their nations further harm.

In addition, Leonor had to confront the question of how her adultery might influence the behavior of others. This element of *noblesse oblige* in Boker's works may distress modern readers, just as his personality may offend some readers. He thought himself superior to the mass of men; and, in the artificial terms of wealth and social position, he was superior. He was, too, a

typical Victorian gentleman who lived an outer life of moral
rectitude and conformity while doing pretty much as he pleased
in private. Our time claims to prize honesty and sincerity and
to despise hypocrisy. The attitude of a man like Boker, or the
attitude of a character like Leonor, may seem to some snobbish
and elitist. Why should Leonor have the luxury both of committing adultery and of troubling herself with whether others ought
to be allowed to do the same thing?

It is important, however, to go beneath this superficial reaction. Boker is not Hawthorne, and nothing in Boker remotely
approaches *The Scarlet Letter.* Yet some of the issues that concern
Hawthorne in that work are also issues that concern Boker.
Some readers resist reading *The Scarlet Letter* as anything other
than a plea for individual liberty and refuse to see that Hawthorne's examination of the effects of the adultery touches not
only on Hester's defiance of convention and her argument that
the adultery sanctified itself, but also on the effects of the adultery
on Hester, on Pearl, and on Dimmesdale. For Boker, the issues
in his plays involve more than an individual's desire for self-
fulfillment. He saw that an individual cannot be reduced to a
single desire. That Leonor worries about the effect of her adultery is not so much snobbishness as it is her recognition that
the adultery did not completely represent her own desires. In
an imperfect world she has had to choose from among imperfect
options. Her fear is that others will see the surface of her behavior and miss the deeper ambiguities. Had Boker presented the
issue otherwise, he would have been naive. At his best, as in
Leonor de Guzman and in his treatment of Francesca and Paolo,
he is no more interested in suggesting that unconventional behavior in and of itself can be equated with self-fulfillment than
he is in suggesting that conformity in and of itself is spiritual
death. What interested Boker was the tension his characters
were forced to explore when one part of their identities conflicted with another.

But considered as romances, Boker's plays fail to exploit the
resources of the romance, and this failure points to his inability,
or unwillingness, to probe fully the issues his works raise. While
the settings of his plays (Calaynos's estate, Henry's court, Medina Sidonia, Seville, the garden in *Francesca da Rimini*) have
thematic significance, the settings remain undeveloped. In his

treatment of Medina Sidonia, for example, Boker invokes the pastoral idea that nature itself is a chaotic wilderness which human effort makes orderly by establishing a garden. At other times, however, nature represents an order for Boker that is in some way superior to the artificial order represented by the city. Yet the details of Boker's descriptions never provide a precise definition of the order nature is to represent. The closest he comes to a full and complex definition is in *Leonor de Guzman,* where he suggests that the pastoral order of Medina Sidonia is in some way synonymous with the order of heaven. But as in *Anne Boleyn,* the concept of heaven, or of what heaven represents, remains vague in *Leonor de Guzman,* particularly if one wishes to examine how this universal moral order revealed itself, as Leonor claims it has, through her adultery.

So, too, other devices which in romance could be made thematically significant are in Boker's works left unexamined. In *Calaynos,* for example, both Lady Alda and Calaynos refer to the portraits of Calaynos's ancestors. In *Francesca da Rimini* Lanciotto describes his childhood experience of seeing a violent death, an experience that causes the mark on his forehead. Both the portraits and Lanciotto's early experience are suggestive devices that have moral and psychological implications that Boker might have explored in order to enrich the thematic complexity, and thus the universal truth, of his works.

But Boker was not, like Hawthorne, skillful enough to make every detail count. He was fond of invoking nature, heaven, and the past, with its overtones of an inexorable fate, not so that he could examine their moral and psychological implications, but so that he could suggest a vague universal order or, in the case of his use of the past, heighten suspense and create a feeling of impending doom. Too often, Boker's devices are suggestive in the bad, rather than the good, sense; and by the last plays he had given over any attempt to make the details of his works (Arbaces' house, the idol of Isis, Nydia's blindness) thematically significant. Indeed, the late plays belong in the tradition of *Ben Hur* and *Gone with the Wind.*

Although after *Francesca da Rimini* Boker's plays become increasingly less significant, he did continue to wrestle with the question of the individual and society. Ironically, having spent most of his career trying to escape his time, Boker found the source of one of his most important works, the *Sonnets: A Sequence on Profane Love,* in his own experience. As his response to his need that someone approve of, and accept, his literary efforts; as a witty and radical inversion of conventional attitudes toward sexual love and religious faith; and as an attempt to revive an older literary tradition, the sonnet sequence belongs among Boker's best works. As yet another example of his inability to create a fully controlled and entirely satisfying work, the sequence is another frustration.

To say that Boker's career is a series of frustrations is not to say that that career is without merit or interest. Given his tendency toward the melodramatic and the problems inherent in his literary method, Boker's successes are the more remarkable. Moreover, in his struggle to realize his literary ambitions he confronted all the difficulties of being a writer in America: he had to define himself and to justify his role in society; he had to define and to justify his literary method; and, although he did not need to earn his living by writing, he nonetheless had to define his relationship with, and his expectations of, his audience. While he did not successfully meet these challenges, Boker did create works that have more than an historical interest. *Anne Boleyn, Leonor de Guzman, Francesca da Rimini,* and the sonnet sequence are more than documents in American literary history. They are as well complex works of literature that touch, even if they never quite adequately reveal, the complex truth of human life.

Notes and References

Chapter One

1. Jay B. Hubbell, "George Henry Boker, Paul Hamilton Hayne, and Charles Warren Stoddard: Some Unpublished Letters," *American Literature* 5 (May 1923): 164.

2. The major sources of information on Boker's life and career are, first, the letters cited parenthetically in the text. The following abbreviations are used throughout the book: LB, Letter from Bayard Taylor to George Henry Boker, Cornell University Library; LES, Letter from George Henry Boker to Elizabeth Stoddard, Princeton University Library; LH, Letter from George Henry Boker to John Seely Hart, Cornell University Library; LS, Letter from George Henry Boker to Richard Henry Stoddard, Princeton University Library; LT, Letter from George Henry Boker to Bayard Taylor, Cornell University Library.

In addition to the letters, the major sources of biographical information are Charles Godfrey Leland's *Memoirs* (1893; rpt. Detroit, 1968) and Edward Sculley Bradley's *George Henry Boker, Poet and Patriot* (Philadelphia, 1927) (hereafter cited as Bradley, *Boker*). In addition, see Richard Henry Stoddard, "Boker and His Letters," *Recollections, Personal and Literary,* ed. R. Hitchcock (New York, 1903), pp. 180–200; Marie Hansen-Taylor with Lilian Bayard Taylor Kiliani, *On Two Continents* (New York, 1905). For a discussion of the Philadelphia society to which Boker belonged, see E. Digby Baltzell, *Philadelphia Gentlemen: The Making of a National Upper Class* (Glencoe, Ill.: Free Press, 1958) and Nathaniel Burt, *The Perennial Philadelphians* (Boston, 1963). John Tomsich's *A Genteel Endeavor* (Stanford, Cal., 1971) discusses Boker as part of the Genteel Tradition. Maxwell Whiteman's *Gentlemen in Crisis* (Philadelphia, 1975) treats Boker's role in the history of the Union League. Paul Wermuth's *Bayard Taylor* (New York, 1973), a study of one of Boker's closest friends, offers an especially illuminating discussion of the importance of both critical and popular success to a writer like Taylor and, as shall be shown here, to Boker. For the stage history of Boker's plays, see J. N. Ireland, *Records of the New York Stage from 1750 to 1860* (1866; rpt. New York: B. Blom, 1966) and Arthur H. Wilson, *A History of the Philadelphia Theatre, 1835 to 1855* (Philadelphia: University of Pennsylvania Press, 1935).

139

For a discussion of the magazines mentioned in chapter 1 and of Boker's relationship with them, see Frank Luther Mott, *A History of American Magazines*. Vols. 1, 2, 3, and 4 (Cambridge: Harvard University Press, 1930–1968).

3. Oliver H. Evans, "Four Letters from George Henry Boker to John Seely Hart," *Pennsylvania Magazine of History and Biography* 104 (January 1980): 43.

4. Leland, *Memoirs*, p. 97.

5. For Boker's account of the events surrounding the essay, see Evans, "Four Letters," pp. 50–51.

6. Charles Brockden Brown, "The Rhapsodist," *The Rhapsodist and Other Uncollected Writings*, ed. H. R. Warfel (New York: Scholars' Facsimiles & Reprints, 1943), p. 10; Henry Theodore Tuckerman, *Mental Portraits; or Studies of Character* (London: R. Bently, 1853), p. 274.

7. Oliver Wendell Holmes, *The Poet at the Breakfast Table* (Boston: Houghton, Mifflin, 1900), p. 99.

8. Leland, *Memoirs*, p. 66.

9. "Ad Criticum," *Konigsmark, The Legend of the Hounds, and Other Poems* (Philadelphia, 1869), p. 199.

10. "Pre-eminence of the Man of Letters," *Nassau Monthly* 2 (January 1843): 76; hereafter page references cited in the text in parentheses.

11. Leland, *Memoirs*, p. 223.

12. Marie Hansen-Taylor, *On Two Continents*, p. 157.

13. Caroline M. Kirkland, "Introductory," *Union Magazine of Literature and Art* 1 (July 1847): 2.

14. *Sartain's Union Magazine* 10 (February 1852): 197.

15. "The Lesson of Life," *The Lesson of Life and Other Poems* (Philadelphia, 1848), p. 13; hereafter page references cited in the text in parentheses.

16. "The Spirit of Poesy," *The Snowflake: A Holiday Gift for 1849* (Philadelphia, 1848), p. 19; hereafter page references cited in the text in parentheses.

17. "The Ivory Carver," *Plays and Poems*, vol. 2 (1856; rpt. New York, 1967), p. 260; hereafter page references cited in the text in parentheses.

18. Champion Bissell, "American Authorship," *Sartain's Union Magazine* 8 (June 1851): 367.

19. Ibid.

20. Arthur Hobson Quinn, "The Dramas of George Henry Boker," *PMLA* 32 (Spring 1917): 266.

21. "Odin," *Nassau Monthly* 2 (September 1842): 25; hereafter page references cited in the text in parentheses.

22. Evans, "Four Letters," p. 55.

23. "Countess Laura," *Königsmark, . . . and Other Poems,* p. 187.

24. "Ad Criticum," ibid., p. 200.

25. Jay B. Hubbell, "Five Letters from George Henry Boker to William Gilmore Simms," *Pennsylvania Magazine of History and Biography* 63 (January 1939): 71.

26. Walt Whitman, Preface to 1855 edition, *Leaves of Grass,* ed. H. W. Boldgett and S. Bradley (New York: New York University Press, 1965), p. 717.

27. Henry Wadsworth Longfellow, *Kavanaugh* (Boston: Houghton, Mifflin, 1904), p. 429.

28. Hubbell, "George Henry Boker," p. 155.

29. Herman Melville, "Hawthorne and His Mosses," *The Portable Melville,* ed. J. Leyda (New York: Viking Press, 1952), p. 411.

30. Erastus Everett, *A System of English Versification* (New York: D. Appleton, 1848), p. 7.

31. Hubbell, "George Henry Boker," p. 160.

32. The review to which Boker refers appeared in the *New York Times,* December 6, 1856, p. 3.

33. See *The North American Review* 84 (January 1857): 268–69.

34. Quoted in Laura Stedman and George M. Gould, *Life and Letters of Edmund Clarence Stedman,* vol. 1 (New York, 1910), p. 329.

35. Bradley, *Boker,* p. 312.

36. Evans, "Four Letters," p. 53.

Chapter Two

1. Donald Clive Stuart, *The Development of Dramatic Art* (1928; rpt. New York: Dover Publications, 1960), p. 510.

2. *Calaynos,* in *Plays and Poems,* vol. 1, p. 31. Page references to *Calaynos, Anne Boleyn,* and *Leonor de Guzman* hereafter cited in the text in parentheses are to this volume.

3. This is the line of interpretation adopted by Bradley; see pp. 50–61.

4. See Antonia Fraser, Introduction to *The Lives of the Kings and Queens of England* (New York: Knopf, 1975), p. 10.

5. See the review of *Anne Boleyn* in *Sartain's Union Magazine* 6 (March 1850): 241–42.

6. Agnes Strickland, *Lives of the Queens of England,* vol. 4 (Boston: Taggard & Thompson, 1864), p. 189.

7. Ibid.

8. Ibid., pp. 144–45.

9. Bradley, *Boker,* p. 77.

10. Hubbell, "Five Letters," p. 71.
11. *The Betrothal,* in *Plays and Poems,* vol. 2, p. 122.
12. Edward Sculley Bradley, Introduction to *Glaucus and Other Plays,* vol. 3 of *America's Lost Plays* (Princeton, 1940), p. xi.
13. *The Bankrupt,* in *Glaucus and Other Plays,* p. 59.
14. *Leonor de Guzman* in *Plays and Poems,* vol. 1, p. 246; hereafter page references given in parentheses in the text.

Chapter Three

1. *Francesca da Rimini, Plays and Poems,* vol. 1, p. 378; hereafter page references given in parentheses in the text.
2. See Paul C. Sherr, "George Henry Boker's *Francesca da Rimini:* A Justification for the Literary Historian," *Pennsylvania History* 34 (October 1967): 361–71, and Paul D. Voelker, "George Henry Boker's *Francesca da Rimini:* An Interpretation and Evaluation," *Educational Theatre Journal* 24 (December 1972): 383–95.
3. *Königsmark,* p. 200.
4. Joseph Wood Krutch, "George Henry Boker: A Little Known American Dramatist," *Sewanee Review* 25 (October 1917): 463.
5. See Jules Zanger, "Boker's *Francesca da Rimini:* The Brothers' Tragedy," *Educational Theatre Journal* 15 (December 1973): 410–19.

Chapter Four

1. *Nydia,* ed. E. S. Bradley (Philadelphia, 1929), p. 101.
2. *The Book of the Dead* (Philadelphia, 1882), p. 18; hereafter page references cited in the text in parentheses.
3. *Poems of the War* (1864; rpt. New York, 1972), p. 48; hereafter page references cited in the text in parentheses.
4. See Bradley, *Boker,* pp. 224–29.
5. *Plays and Poems,* vol. 2, p. 401; hereafter page references to these sonnets cited in the text in parentheses.
6. Edward Sculley Bradley, "George Henry Boker and Angie Hicks," *American Literature* 8 (November 1936): 258–65.
7. Ibid., p. 262.
8. Quoted in Tomsich, *Genteel Endeavor,* p. 160.
9. As noted earlier, 281 sonnets were written to Angie Hicks. The first sequence consists of 282 sonnets because in his manuscript Boker indicated that one of the sonnets from the second sequence should be placed first in a book were the sonnets published. See *Sonnets: A Sequence on Profane Love,* ed. E. S. Bradley (Philadelphia, 1929), p. 17.

10. *A Sequence on Profane Love,* p. 78; hereafter the sonnets are cited by number in the text.

11. Stoddard, *Recollections,* p. 275.

12. Herman Melville, *Pierre; or, The Ambiguities, The Writings of Herman Melville,* vol. 7, Northwestern-Newberry Edition, ed. H. Hayford et al. (Evanston and Chicago: Northwestern University Press and The Newberry Library, 1971), p. 246.

13. James Fenimore Cooper, *The American Democrat,* ed. G. Dekker and L. Johnston (Baltimore: Penguin Books, 1969), p. 129.

14. Bayard Taylor, *Critical Essays and Literary Notes* (New York: G. P. Putnam's Sons, 1880), p. 244. Significantly, such poets as Emerson and Whitman resolved the tension of the poet's relationship with the public by democratizing the poetic vision and thus making all people potentially poets.

15. Bayard Taylor, *Poetical Works,* Household Edition (1880; rpt. New York: AMS Press, 1970), p. 68.

16. See Robert K. Martin, *The Homosexual Tradition in American Poetry* (Austin: University of Texas Press, 1979), pp. 97–109.

17. See e.g., Richmond Beatty, *Bayard Taylor: Laureate of the Gilded Age* (Norman: University of Oklahoma Press, 1936), pp. 288–90, and Paul Wermuth, *Bayard Taylor,* pp. 94–99. Beatty, imagining what Freudians, "those supremely clever gentlemen" (p. 288), would have made of Taylor's psychology, builds, even as he seeks to demolish, a Freudian portrait of Taylor as a latent homosexual troubled by unresolved Oedipal feelings and disgusted by Swinburne and Whitman, two poets who openly expressed emotions Taylor struggled to repress. Nonetheless, Beatty concludes that suggestions of Taylor's being homosexual—a word, incidentally, Beatty never uses—are "not a little disgusting" and that Taylor "was quite healthy, quite safe, and for his day quite normal" (p. 290). Wermuth, recognizing that "the suggestions of homosexuality [in *Joseph and His Friend*] can hardly be overlooked," concludes that while "scenes of [men] embracing and kissing each other make the reader somewhat uncomfortable, . . . it is by no means certain that the book should be interpreted that way" (p. 97), leaving it unclear whether "that way" refers to the homosexual interpretation or to the reader's discomfort. While less homophobic than Beatty's, Wermuth's argument leads him to claim on one page that "the type of relationship that is depicted in the novel was more normal in the nineteenth century than today" (p. 98) and then to claim a page later that "in the 1970's, such a theme would hardly excite notice, but for 1869 it seems daring" (p. 99). Yet it is a critic in the 1970s who finds Taylor's novel "somewhat uncomfortable," and how comfortable the nineteenth century was with the book is an open question since, as Wermuth says, the book was Taylor's "most

intensely disliked novel" (p. 94). Beatty's argument, to the extent it
can be taken seriously, raises the question of what "quite normal"
meant in the nineteenth century as opposed to now. In short, then,
the argument that male relationships were viewed in an essentially
different way in the nineteenth, as opposed to the twentieth, century
is ultimately unsatisfactory.

18. A possibility raised by Martin, *The Homosexual Tradition*, p.
103.

Chapter Five

1. All quotations from Shakespeare's plays are from *Complete
Plays and Poems,* The New Cambridge Edition (Cambridge, Mass.:
Houghton Mifflin, 1942).

2. *The Journals and Miscellaneous Notebooks of Ralph Waldo Emerson,* ed. W. H. Gilman and J. E. Parsons, vol. 8 (Cambridge, Mass.:
Belknap Press, 1970), p. 400.

3. Ibid.

4. Nathaniel Hawthorne, Preface to *The Blithedale Romance,* in
vol. 3 of Centenary Edition of the Works of Nathaniel Hawthorne,
ed. William Charvat et al. (Columbus: Ohio State University Press,
1964), p. 2. Further references to Hawthorne's works are to this
edition.

5. Taylor, *Critical Essays,* p. 234.

6. Hawthorne, Preface to *The Blithedale Romance,* p. 1.

7. Nathaniel Hawthorne, Preface to *The House of the Seven Gables,*
vol. 2 of the Centenary Edition (Columbus, 1965), p. 1.

8. Hawthorne, Preface to *The Blithedale Romance,* p. 2.

9. Hawthorne, Preface to *The House of the Seven Gables,* p. 2.

10. Charles Godfrey Leland, "The Romantic in Literature and
Art," *Sartain's Union Magazine* 5 (November 1849): 302.

11. Nathaniel Hawthorne, "The Custom House—Introductory,"
The Scarlet Letter, vol. 1 of the Centenary Edition (Columbus, 1962),
p. 36.

12. Richard Chase, *The American Novel and Its Tradition* (Garden
City, N. Y.: Doubleday, 1957), p. 20.

Selected Bibliography

PRIMARY SOURCES

The following list is divided into three groups: poetical works, which includes both Boker's dramas and his poems; essays, which includes only his important college essays; and manuscript materials. The arrangement within the first two groups is chronological by date of publication. No attempt has been made to give the original place of publication for all of Boker's poems; for a partial listing of the original places of publication of some of them, particularly those published during the Civil War, see the bibliography in Bradley's *George Henry Boker, Poet and Patriot.*

1. Poetical Works

The Lesson of Life and Other Poems. Philadelphia: George S. Appleton, 1848.

Calaynos. Philadelphia: E. H. Butler, 1848. Reprinted in *Plays and Poems.*

"The Spirit of Poesy." In *The Snowflake: A Holiday Gift for 1849.* Philadelphia: E. H. Butler, 1848, pp. 13–24.

Anne Boleyn. Philadelphia: A. Hart, 1850. Reprinted in *Plays and Poems.*

The Podesta's Daughter and Other Poems. Philadelphia: A. Hart, 1852. Reprinted in *Plays and Poems.*

Plays and Poems. 2 vols. Boston: Ticknor and Fields, 1856; Reprint. 1857; Reprint. Philadelphia: J. B. Lippincott, 1869; Reprint. 1883; Reprint. 1891; Reprint. New York: AMS Press, 1967. Volume 1 includes four tragedies: *Calaynos, Anne Boleyn, Leonor de Guzman,* and *Francesca da Rimini;* volume 2 includes two comedies—*The Betrothal* and *The Widow's Marriage*—and the poems.

Poems of the War. Boston: Ticknor & Fields, 1864; Reprint. Philadelphia: J. B. Lippincott, 1891; Reprint. New York: Arno Press, 1972.

The Book of the Sonnet. Edited by L. Hunt and S. A. Lee. 2 vols. Boston: Roberts Brothers, 1867. Boker, as well as Paul Hamilton Hayne, contributed to the essay on American sonneteers, vol. 1, pp. 95–131.

Königsmark, The Legend of the Hounds, and Other Poems. Philadelphia:
    J. B. Lippincott, 1869.
The Book of the Dead. Philadelphia: J. B. Lippincott, 1882.
Sonnets: A Sequence on Profane Love. Edited by E. S. Bradley. Philadel-
    phia: University of Pennsylvania Press, 1929.
Nydia. Edited by E. S. Bradley. Philadelphia: University of Pennsylva-
    nia Press, 1929.
Glaucus and Other Plays. Edited by E. S. Bradley. Vol. 3 of *America's
    Lost Plays.* Princeton: Princeton University Press, 1940. Includes
    Glaucus, The World a Mask, and *The Bankrupt.*

2. College Essays
"Norse Poetry." *The Nassau Monthly* 1 (August 1842): 161–66.
"Odin." *The Nassau Monthly* 2 (September 1842): 24–27.
"Pre-eminence of the Man of Letters." *The Nassau Monthly* 2 (January
    1843): 74–79.
"The Faerie Queene." The Nassau Monthly 2 (June 1843): 193–201.

3. Manuscript Materials
The major collection of Boker's papers is at Princeton University and
    includes his manuscripts as well as typed transcripts of 102 letters
    to Richard Henry Stoddard (AM 13875). Other Boker material,
    including a second manuscript of the sonnet sequence, is at the
    University of Pennsylvania Library. The Boker-Taylor correspon-
    dence (187 letters from Taylor to Boker; 164 from Boker to
    Taylor) is at the Cornell University Library, as are thirty-nine
    letters from Boker to John Seely Hart.

SECONDARY SOURCES

1. Books and Parts of Books
Bradley, Edward Sculley. *George Henry Boker, Poet and Patriot.* Phila-
    delphia: University of Pennsylvania Press, 1927; Reprint. New
    York: AMS Press, 1969. A biographical and critical study that
    finds Boker a great poet destroyed by neglect. Interprets the plays
    solely in terms of a noble individual thwarted by a corrupt society.
    The book remains a useful discussion of Boker's life, and its treat-
    ment of Boker's manuscripts and the stage history of his plays
    is thorough.

Burt, Nathaniel. *The Perennial Philadelphians: The Anatomy of an American Aristocracy.* Boston: Little, Brown, 1963. Less reverential than Bradley, Burt views Boker as "the perfect representative of the Philadelphia fatality, universally favored in his outward fortunes," but "utterly forgotten, after a modest lifetime reputation."

Hansen-Taylor, Marie, and **Horace E. Scudder,** eds. *Life and Letters of Bayard Taylor.* 2 vols. Boston: Houghton, Mifflin, 1884. Includes many letters from Taylor to Boker.

————, with the cooperation of Lilian Bayard Taylor Kiliani. *On Two Continents: Memoirs of Half a Century.* New York: Doubleday, Page, 1905. While the book's focus is Taylor, its glimpses into the literary life of Boker's time are fascinating.

Leland, Charles Godfrey. *Memoirs.* New York: D. Appleton, 1893; rpt. Detroit: Gale Research Company, 1968. Written by one of Boker's closest friends, and one who knew him from childhood, the book is an important source of material.

Pennell, Elizabeth Robins. *Charles Godfrey Leland.* 2 vols. Boston: Houghton, Mifflin, 1906. Includes extracts from Boker's letters to Leland.

Quinn, Arthur Hobson. "George Henry Boker and the Later Romantic Tragedy." In *A History of the American Drama from the Beginning to the Civil War.* New York: Harper and Brothers, 1923, pp. 337–67. A standard work on American drama and, with Bradley's biography, a basic work on Boker.

Stedman, Laura, and **George M. Gould.** *Life and Letters of Edmund Clarence Stedman.* 2 vols. New York: Moffat, Yard, 1910. Includes a letter from Boker to Stedman (vol. 1, p. 329) as well as Stedman's letter inviting Boker to join the Authors Club (vol. 2, pp. 464–65).

Stoddard, Richard Henry. "Boker and His Letters." In *Recollections, Personal and Literary.* Edited by R. Hitchcock. New York: A. S. Barnes, 1903, pp. 180–200. Originally written shortly after Boker's death, the "recollection" outlines his career and assesses his work.

Tomsich, John. *A Genteel Endeavor: American Culture and Politics in the Gilded Age.* Stanford: Stanford University Press, 1971. A study of eight important figures in the Genteel Tradition: Thomas Bailey Aldrich, Richard Henry Stoddard, Charles Eliot Norton, Edmund Clarence Stedman, Bayard Taylor, Richard Watson Gilder, George William Curtis, and George Henry Boker.

Wermuth, Paul C. *Bayard Taylor.* New York: Twayne Publishers, 1973. A study of one of Boker's closest friends.

Whiteman, Maxwell. *Gentlemen in Crisis: The First Century of the Union League of Philadelphia, 1862–1962.* Philadelphia: The Union League of Philadelphia, 1975. A thorough discussion of Boker's role in the League.

2. Articles

Beatty, Richmond C. "Bayard Taylor and George Henry Boker." *American Literature* 6 (November 1934): 316–27. Concludes that the two were friends and influenced each other; quotes extensively from the Boker-Taylor correspondence.

Bradley, Edward Sculley. "George Henry Boker and Angie Hicks." *American Literature* 8 (November 1936): 258–65. Identifies Angelina (King) Hicks as the woman addressed in many of Boker's sonnets.

————. A Newly Discovered American Sonnet Sequence." *PMLA* 40 (Winter 1925): 910–20. The points made here are repeated in Bradley's biography of Boker as well as in the introduction to Bradley's edition of the sequence.

————. "Poe on the New York Stage in 1855." *American Literature* 9 (November 1937): 353–54. Discusses the mention of Poe in *The Bankrupt* and the influence of Poe's M. Dupin on Boker's Pike.

Burt, Nathaniel. "Chauvinism, Princeton and Genteel Poets." *Princeton University Library Chronicle* 25 (Spring 1964): 179–83. Sees a " 'Princeton literary tradition,' anchored in Freneau, established in Boker and moving on through John Peale Bishop."

Evans, Oliver H. "Four Letters from George Henry Boker to John Seely Hart." *Pennsylvania Magazine of History and Biography* 104 (January 1980): 39–57. The letters, the last four in the Cornell collection, are dated November 4, 1874; January 31, 1875; April 7, 1875; and October 23, 1875.

————. "George Henry Boker's 'The Spirit of Poesy.' " *American Notes & Queries* 18 (May 1980): 140–41. Discusses the manuscript and the publication of this early Boker poem.

————. "Shakespearean Prototypes and the Failure of Boker's *Francesca da Rimini.*" *Educational Theatre Journal* 30 (May 1978): 211–19. Argues that Boker fails to integrate his borrowings from Shakespeare and is thus unable to make Lanciotto either consistent or intelligible.

Flory, Claude R. "Boker, Barrett and the Francesca Theme in Drama." *Players: Magazine of American Theatre* 50 (February–March, 1975): 58–61, 80. Compares Barrett's acting version with the published version of *Francesca da Rimini.*

Gallagher, Kent G. "The Tragedies of George Henry Boker: The Measure of American Romantic Tragedy." *ESQ: A Journal of the American Renaissance* 20 (3rd Quarter 1974): 187–215. Distinguishes Boker's romantic dramas from those of his predecessors and traces his development from *Calaynos* to *Francesca da Rimini*.

Hubbell, Jay B. "Five Letters from George Henry Boker to William Gilmore Simms." *Pennsylvania Magazine of History and Biography* 63 (January 1939): 66–71. The letters, all from 1869, are dated January 5; September 9; September 22; November 11; and December 24.

————. "George Henry Boker, Paul Hamilton Hayne, and Charles Warren Stoddard: Some Unpublished Letters." *American Literature* 5 (May 1933): 146–65. Includes one letter from Boker to Hayne dated April 15, 1867; and six letters from Boker to Stoddard dated August 12, 1867; November 30, 1867; February 9, 1868; June 29, 1868; September 7, 1868; and September 9, 1869.

Kincaid, Arthur Noel. "Italian and English Sources of Boker's *Francesca da Rimini* (1853)." *American Transcendental Quarterly* 1 (1st Quarter 1969): 91–100. Concludes that only Dante and Boccaccio influenced Boker.

Krutch, Joseph Wood. "George Henry Boker: A Little Known American Dramatist." *Sewanee Review* 25 (October 1917): 457–68. An early and influential study of Boker as the climactic figure in the development of romantic tragedy.

Leland, Charles Godfrey. "Boker's Plays." *Sartain's Union Magazine* 8 (June 1851): 369–78. Particularly good discussion of *Anne Boleyn*.

Metcalf, J. C. "An Old Romantic Triangle: *Francesca da Rimini* in Three Dramas." *Sewanee Review* 29 (January 1921): 45–58. A comparison of Boker's play with those by the English playwright Stephen Phillips and the Italian Gabriele D'Annunzio.

Quinn, Arthur Hobson. "The Dramas of George Henry Boker." *PMLA* 32 (Spring 1917): 233–66. Later incorporated in Quinn's *History of American Drama*.

————. "George Henry Boker, Playwright and Patriot." *Scribner's Magazine* 73 (June 1923): 701–15. A survey of Boker's life and career.

Requa, Kenneth A. "George Henry Boker." *American Literary Realism, 1870–1910* 8 (Summer 1975): 201–3. A review, mostly negative, of dissertations on Boker.

Sherr, Paul C. "George Henry Boker's *Francesca da Rimini:* A Justification for the Literary Historian." *Pennsylvania History* 34 (October

1967): 361–71. A reading of the play in terms of "Boker's personal frustrations."

Shuman, R. Baird. "A Note on George Boker's *Francesca da Rimini.*" *American Literature* 31 (January 1960): 480–82. Prints a letter from Boker to a Mrs. Johnson, otherwise unidentified, September 7, 1882, that establishes Dante and Boccaccio as the sources of *Francesca da Rimini.*

Stewart, Patricia L. "The Influence of Thomas More on the Early American Stage." *Moreana* 51 (September 1976): 132–38. Argues that *Anne Boleyn* reveals Boker's attitude toward More.

Urban, Gertrude. "Paolo and Francesca in History and Literature." *Critic* 40 (May 1902): 425–38. A discussion of the Francesca material.

Voelker, Paul D. "George Henry Boker's *Francesca da Rimini:* An Interpretation and Evaluation." *Educational Theatre Journal* 24 (December 1972): 383–95. The play treats two noble individuals crushed by a corrupt society.

Woods, Alan. "Producing Boker's *Francesca da Rimini.*" *Educational Theatre Journal* 24 (December 1972): 396–401. An account of a production given at the University of Southern California, Los Angeles, in April 1972.

Zanger, Jules. "Boker's *Francesca da Rimini:* The Brothers' Tragedy." *Educational Theatre Journal* 25 (December 1973): 410–19. Discusses Boker's addition of the fraternal love theme to the traditional story.

Index

Taylor, Marie, 8
Taylor, Mary Agnew, 115
Thackeray, William M., 90
Thoreau, Henry D., 10
Ticknor and Fields, 21, 90, 126
Tuckerman, Henry Theodore, 5
Twelfth Night (Shakespeare), 53
"Twin Love" (Taylor), 117

Union Magazine of Literature and Art, 10

Views A-Foot (Taylor), 9

Walden (Thoreau), 2
Walker, Sears C., 2
Wallace, Lew, 135, 137
War poems, 124
Whitman, Walt, 10, 17, 19, 100, 121
Willis, Nathaniel Park, 111, 112
Wordsworth's description of Dante's sonnets, 118
Wyatt, Thomas, 39, 123
Wylie, Elinor, 106, 107

Yeats, W. B., 107